Going
Against
the
Grain

CORWIN
PRESS

The Corwin Press logo—a raven striding across an open book—represents the happy union of courage and learning. We are a professional-level publisher of books and journals for K-12 educators, and we are committed to creating and providing resources that embody these qualities. Corwin's motto is "Success for All Learners."

Going Against the Grain

Supporting the Student-Centered Teacher

Elizabeth Aaronsohn

CORWIN PRESS, INC.
A Sage Publications Company
Thousand Oaks, California

For information address:

Corwin Press, Inc.
A Sage Publications Company
2455 Teller Road
Thousand Oaks, California 91320
E-mail: order@corwin.sagepub.com

SAGE Publications Ltd.
6 Bonhill Street
London EC2A 4PU
United Kingdom

SAGE Publications India Pvt. Ltd.
M-32 Market
Greater Kailash I
New Delhi 110 048 India

Printed in the United States of America

Library of Congress Cataloging-in-Publication Data

Aaronsohn, Elizabeth.
    Going against the grain: Supporting the student-centered teacher
/ author, Elizabeth Aaronsohn.
        p.   cm.
    Includes bibliographical references and index.
    ISBN 0-8039-6297-5 (cloth: acid-free).   —   ISBN 0-8039-6298-3
(pbk.: acid free)
        1. Mentoring in education—United States—Case studies.
    2. Student teachers—Training of—United States—Case studies.
    3. Teacher-student relationships—United States—Case studies.
    4. Active learning—United States—Case studies.   I. Title.
    LB1731.4.A27 1996
    370'.71'23—dc20   95-32535

This book is printed on acid-free paper.

95 96 97 98 99 10 9 8 7 6 5 4 3 2 1

Corwin Press Project Editor: Christina M. Hill

Contents

About the Author

Elizabeth Aaronsohn is Assistant Professor in the Department of Teacher Education at Central Connecticut State University. Having returned to graduate school for her doctoral studies in Teacher Education at age 50, she speaks of herself now as being in her second 30-year career. In her first, she taught 8 years each at three levels: high school English, college English, and elementary school. Outside the formal system, she taught and learned as a peace and justice activist, teacher/coordinator of the Mississippi Freedom Schools, educational director for a religious school, and mother. She learned about mentoring by being generously mentored through graduate school. She considers her best preparation for student-centered teaching to have been her many waitressing jobs, and time spent gardening. Most especially, she gives credit for her teaching philosophies to the peace and justice movements, through which she learned to examine her own traditional schooling and early teaching, and within which she is still growing to understand and cherish community. Teaching more like Sheila since 1990, her other main areas of research include multicultural education, the effects of traditional grading on authentic learning, and dialoguing for student reflectiveness. The story told in *Going Against the Grain* includes part of the evolution of Dr. Aaronsohn as participant researcher, teacher educator, and activist passionately committed to people-centered democratic processes.

1 Supporting Student-Centered Teaching

Preservice teachers keep asking the question, "If so much is known about what is good teaching, why isn't that kind of teaching happening in the schools? We read about actively buzzing classrooms in which children explore and engage with materials and with one another to construct their own meaning. Then, when we go out to the field, we still see the same kinds of silent, boring, teacher-centered, workbook-driven classrooms we used to think were the only possible models. How can we expect to go out and do all these exciting things if no one else in the school is doing them?"

Teacher educators and researchers ask a pair of companion questions: How can we find enough models of the practices that we advocate for our preservice teachers to observe and with whom to student teach? What can be done to keep new teachers, who envision themselves teaching in constructivist and student-centered ways, from being swallowed up by the traditional cultures of the schools once they leave the university?

This book may serve as a complex response to those recurrent questions. It suggests that if practicing teachers have direct continuing access to teacher educators for support while they and their students work at letting go of traditional assumptions, then perhaps

1

people who dare to imagine transformed, student-centered teaching[1] can work freely, if gradually, toward their vision.

The Structure of the Book

Although the book concludes with voices of many teachers, their experiences serve to reinforce and translate the conclusions drawn from the story of Sheila,[2] a high school English teacher who overcame internal and external pressures as she grew to experience and then claim her own effectiveness as a student-centered teacher. Perceiving many of her colleagues' comments and behaviors as pressure to doubt her vision, Sheila's struggle was ultimately toward living her own definition of "good teaching." The description of that struggle portrays the crucial function of a teacher educator's support for one teacher. The support was regular, personal, and nonjudgmental. It was on-site but not invested in the culture of the school.

From both my readings and my previous experience as a teacher and a teacher educator, I had predicted the usefulness of such support. It had not, however, occurred to me how pivotal the relationship would be for the teacher to feel empowered to choose his or her own direction in spite of all the pressures he or she felt. Nor had I foreseen the extent to which the process of the mentoring relationship would parallel the process of student-centered teaching.

This study found that it did make a difference in the confidence of the teacher in the study, in the quality of her instruction, and in her satisfaction and others' satisfaction with student learning when the teacher received intensive personal support from a university teacher educator. It therefore suggests a need for reconceptualization of both teaching and teacher education; otherwise, traditional pedagogies that disempower both students and teachers will inevitably continue to prevail, despite the overwhelming contraindication of research evidence and the good intentions of teacher educators.

Because my personal bias as adviser in this study was a commitment to student-centered teaching, my participation in Sheila's growth in this form of instruction was not simply that of witness and reliable recorder. My presence constituted a deliberate intervention, which consisted almost entirely of active listening as Sheila talked through her experiences and her needs. My sharing of her vision allowed her to see me as a resource who could understand and extend her thinking, even as I was providing a vehicle for her reflection.

The work was not unrelievedly successful. Some of the role tensions I had anticipated were present: mirror, listener, teacher educator, mentor, friend, advocate of student-centered teaching, and researcher. There were others that I had not predicted. For example, during a long initial period, Sheila felt apprehensive that she could not live up to what she perceived to be my expectations of her. Although her doubts recurred periodically after that time, she ultimately came to trust that my intention was not to pressure her toward choices that felt inconsistent with her own vision.

Essentially, we had chosen one another as colleagues. I needed to observe a teacher who would be operating from the assumption that students, with one another, can and should generate their own learning. She needed a mentor for the student-centered and cooperative-learning strategies she had decided to try. This case study, then, provides the connecting point between the theory and the practice of student-centered teaching.

Throughout the data, the theme of teaching as a nurturing relationship recurs most compellingly. What emerges is that the attitudes and approaches that seem effective in supporting a student-centered teacher are, in many ways, the attitudes and approaches that are effective in conducting a student-centered classroom. The clear finding of this study is that if high school teachers are to be nurturers of students in their classrooms, they must receive the kind of regular support that hears, knows, validates, and helps them grow in their work.

Context: The School

Although Valley Central Regional High School (VCRHS) had begun to make a long-range effort toward completely heterogeneously grouped classes just before Sheila was hired to teach there, as a later chapter will show, the reality was somewhat more complex. During the first year of the study, her first year at the school, Sheila traveled between several classrooms to conduct her courses. In the second year, she had her own room and supplied and decorated it in a manner that represented her personal and professional tastes and interests as well as her sense of what would appeal to and inspire students.

One wall lined with bookshelves contained hundreds of diverse paperback and hardcover novels, which Sheila had gathered for their potential appeal to students who were encouraged to borrow or even keep them. Another wall displayed student writing and projects, highlighted by large, colorful lettering identifying the assignments. Strategically placed cartoons and posters reminded students to think positive thoughts and to dare to take risks. Several photographs and paintings of irises, Sheila's favorite flower, added a gentle personal touch to the displays.

Summary of Sheila's Story

Sheila began her first year of teaching English at VCRHS in the fall of 1988. Having accepted this job and, in fact, having been told she had been chosen for it because of her commitment to the school's newly stated policy of heterogeneous grouping, she had felt ready with strategies that had worked for her in her previous teaching.

She came with an admittedly nontraditional set of beliefs about teaching high school English: that students are capable of working responsibly when they are asked to work cooperatively; that they can learn what they need to learn about writing and even grammar through projects and the writing of journals and reader-response papers; and that they can, without much overt direction from the teacher, individually and collaboratively work at discovering for themselves the meanings in a literary text.

Immediately, in the first week of September, she found herself in an unexpected collision with student resistance to the interactive processes she was trying to introduce. Worse, she was devastated by colleagues' scoffing at her beliefs. It was not what the students expected; it was not what the other teachers were doing. Maybe it was not the right thing to do. Comparing her own work with what she understood the other teachers in the building to be doing, she felt confused.

The prevailing ethic in this context at VCRHS seemed to be traditional academic performance. In her previous teaching, working with so-called "low-achieving" students for whom there had been little pressure toward college, she had essentially been allowed to define her own success. Her vision of young people coming to hear and trust their own voices had been realized in those earlier situations.

Now she was asking herself whether her previously successful focus on classroom community building, relationship, self-esteem, and personal interaction with texts was inappropriate for these classes in this school. Were those approaches and that freedom good only for elementary students, or only for high school students in whose academic success nobody seemed to believe? Listening to other teachers and to the students themselves, she was apprehensive. Would her students get what they "needed" if she did not accommodate to the teaching norm? Would she have to rethink her values, expectations, and hopes for her students? Sheila's sense of her professional self was deeply shaken.

Deprived of the approval of her colleagues and department chair and of the active support of the principal, Sheila allowed a teacher educator who shared her values and vision of teaching to help her gain perspective about her situation. The support of that relationship gave her a means to examine all of the pressures, internal and external, that were keeping her from achieving her vision. In practical terms, it gave her specific feedback that allowed her to try new strategies for fully realizing the student-centered teaching for which she had understood she had been hired at VCRHS. Increasingly, with that support, she began to take risks with both the content and the pedagogy of her classroom and to speak out within the building when she perceived that students' real needs, as she defined them, were not being addressed.

Her progress toward finding her own way with student-centered teaching suffered a setback during the semester in which she team-taught one senior English course with the department chair Ralph, whose approval she sought. During that fall 1989 semester, because of both the frequency of contact and his position of authority, she felt compelled to follow his lead in her own teaching, at least in the team-taught class.

In so drastically changing her own approach, however, she had not counted on the rebellion of students who, having been with her the year before as juniors, had adjusted to and flourished under her earlier teaching. Their reaction intensified her struggle. She again saw and felt herself to be an outcast as she had the year before. Part of her still wanted very much to fit in. Nevertheless, when she refocused on the students, she realized, "I've betrayed the kids by doing it Ralph's way." But an adequate alternative course of action was not yet clear to her: "I'm not sure my way is better."

The result of Sheila's personal and professional struggle at VCRHS to become the kind of teacher she deeply wanted to be was apparent. In less than 2 full academic years, she was able to assert with confidence that her preferred way of teaching was, in fact, better for her students. Her focus was redirected to the students as she let go of caring whether colleagues accepted her or even if the students liked her. Conscious of that difference in her approach, she finally came to believe that she was teaching better than she had ever taught before.

As she claimed her own power, colleagues began to seek her out for feedback on their own work and to admire hers. As she had done in previous schools, she expanded her interest in her students' lives to include parents, the school committee, the community, and colleagues in other schools, many of whom now praised her for her energetic commitment to heterogeneous grouping and student empowerment. The administrators of the school and the district recognized her work. More important to Sheila, the seniors invited her to be their speaker in graduation week's senior chapel. In her speech to the graduating seniors, she told them what her teaching had been telling both them and herself for 2 years: Believe in yourselves, love one another, and have the courage to live according to your consciences. By the end of the 2-year study, she was sure of what she wanted to do and could do and was looking at what she needed to learn in order to do it even better.

The process of Sheila's arrival at a clear sense of who she wanted to be as a teacher can perhaps be described as her gradual release of needs and expectations that got in the way of focusing on the real needs and real abilities of the individuals and groups in her classes. The transformation of Sheila was a spiral, not a linear, process. Her vision was shaken by her need for the approval of colleagues and the department chair, her ambivalence about what she should be doing, her feeling of fundamental difference from most of the people who seemed to be criticizing her, and her thoughts of what she must do when the struggle tired her.

This book will describe the process of Sheila's becoming, in reality, a student-centered teacher. The meaning of this will be analyzed in depth, through her own voice and through glimpses of her classroom. The final chapter of her story will document the reinforcement of her original vision by a 2-year relationship with a university teacher educator/mentor who shared that vision. The data suggest that her growth in confidence was directly connected to her taking the enormous risk of allowing the ownership of the classroom and what happens in it to be shared daily with the students and, for a time, regularly with an observer. As Sheila described it, the presence of the teacher educator as mentor in her professional life served as a persistent reminder of her commitment to the kind of teaching that puts students at the center of learning.

Origins of the Study

The particular set of questions that underlay my interest in Sheila's story as a research study grew out of my own direct experience of being a K-12 classroom teacher for 17 years, followed by several years of observing and attempting to support student teachers as they became socialized into their complex profession. The study comes from both experiencing and witnessing the tension, confusion, and even despair suffered by new teachers who found themselves caught between university teacher education courses, in which they had studied innovative methods designed to empower students, and a set of so-called "institutional realities" that made the implementation of those methods seem inappropriate or impossible.

For much of my own teaching career, I have been working to figure out for myself how to teach—and recently how to help others learn to teach—in a student-centered rather than in a teacher-centered way. My own experience, reinforced by research, overwhelmingly shows that more complex, more long-lasting, and more whole learning take place when students are active rather than passive learners, when they engage with the material rather than just passively absorbing it, and especially when they can interact with one another in the classroom. But it is not easy for people socialized within the traditional framework—as most teachers, including myself, have been—to redefine the role of a teacher to allow students to participate fully in their own learning process.

The guiding questions emerged from indications that, as the more thoughtful reform reports maintain, the problem with high schools in the United States is not so much that high school graduates do not score well on standardized tests but that they do not become people who think creatively or divergently, see themselves as competent problem solvers, read and write intelligently or with pleasure, know or care about the world, or see themselves as making change in the world. They do not even have the skills necessary to get along with one another (Tyson, 1994; see also Goodlad, 1990; Haberman, 1992).

If students are to be competent, reflective, decision-making, and caring people, their teachers must both model behaviors reflecting those characteristics and help students develop them. That is the kind of teacher that Sheila wanted to be and knew she could be, and that I wanted to support. As it turned out, the very structure of qualitative research methodology contributed to Sheila's growth in confidence. That should not have been surprising, given the wide understanding in the literature of the importance of concrete feedback to teacher reflection. The frequent, regular, in-depth, unstructured interviews by a person who had no investment in the school allowed her full freedom to talk through all her uncertainties as well as to reconfirm her vision.

The Theoretical Framework

Teacher Development

An ongoing conversation in the teacher education literature attempts to understand why new teachers, whether consciously or unconsciously, tend to teach the way that they perceive they are expected to teach, regardless of the liberal views they may have adopted during college (Blase, 1988; Ross, 1986; Tabachnick & Zeichner, 1984; Wells, 1984). A growing body of research recommends support for practicing teachers: "It may be that . . . there is a need for longitudinal studies that follow student teachers into their early years of teaching" (Zeichner & Liston, 1987, p. 45).

Examining the extent to which internal and contextual factors contribute to teacher conservatism, Blase (1988, pp. 130-131) names certain factors that affect teachers even beyond induction:

- Teachers feel vulnerable to the judgment and power of administrators, parents, and the community.
- They feel isolated from one another.

- They feel overworked.
- They tend to focus on the immediacy of the day-to-day inter-actions with their classes.

In their isolation and vulnerability, even some long-term practicing teachers do not have the time, energy, or inclination to think of themselves as change agents and, in fact, tend to resist being asked to operate in ways that are substantially different from those that have been effective for them (Sarason, 1982). This is especially true if the changes require them to do more than they are already doing or to risk not doing things as well as they have learned to do them, even for a while. The discomfort of uncertainty, especially of seeming uncertain in front of their students or their colleagues, is an added stress that most teachers choose to avoid (Floden & Clark, 1988).

The intervention of teacher educators at this point, therefore, may be critical. Several studies lay out the optimal conditions for that intervention. The need is for on-site, practical, humane, personal, regular, individualized, responsive, nonjudgmental, nonevaluative, and meaningful advising that is supportive and nurturing (Newman, 1980). Individual mentoring, in spite of its labor-intensiveness, provides important aspects of relationship: the adviser's consistent availability over time, concrete situations in the classroom as the basis of conversation, and the adviser's acting as a sounding board in a relationship of mutuality without an overlay of power (Katz, Morpurgo, Asper, & Wolf, 1974).

Even in such an optimal situation, it took almost the entire first year of sustained reflection together for Sheila and me to realize how pervasively the system she was challenging was within as well as outside of her. Thus the information that resulted in this study could result in transforming teacher education. The work of supporting student-centered teachers will take time because a part of the collision may be within a teacher's belief system: between conscious research- and experience-based professional choices on the one hand and deeply ingrained behaviors based on early experience and unexamined assumptions on the other hand.

It would be appropriate, then, to have preservice teachers develop the habit of reflection that dredges up and examines deep-seated assumptions before they find themselves playing fixed, pre-established roles. If even progressive teacher educators deal only with traditional content-centered material, allowing certification courses to be a matter of socializing new teachers into the conventional techniques of their craft, we will be left to hope that teachers will on their own develop complex dispositions fundamental to student-centered curriculum design and classroom management. Along with the acquisition of skills that most new teachers think they need and should be taught (Blase, 1987; Haberman, 1992), preservice teachers must at least have sustained opportunity to confront their own deep assumptions about teaching and learning, and in-service teachers who commit to student-centeredness must be provided with follow-up support, especially if they see almost nothing but their former, traditional preconceptions reinforced in the culture of the schools.

Redefinition of Teaching

The question of whether content or process is to be emphasized in a classroom, or even whether process is worth considering at all at the high school level, seems to underlie the collision between nontraditional teachers and most other high school teachers and, in fact, between a teacher and him- or herself. Even on the elementary school level, decisions about how to make time within a school day for social, moral, and emotional growth and also for preparation for standardized tests are the source of much tension for teachers. This is true even though most elementary school teachers at least enter the profession seeing themselves as nurturers of children's healthy social and emotional development as well as their acquisition of academic skills. If it is hard to manage at that early level, how will it be possible to do it at the secondary and university levels? What is the result if we do not?

An earlier unpublished study, *The Process Is the Content* (Aaronsohn, 1988), attempted to understand through observation and interviews with high school teachers and student teachers why high school teachers are reluctant to use cooperative learning. Its essential finding was that teachers' perceptions of a well-established role that they must play—teacher- and content-centered—exert a profound pressure against their allowing students to generate their own knowledge.

Substantial theoretical grounding exists, however, for defining the role of a teacher—even a high school teacher—in such a way that the professional attention is on the student rather than on the content or on the teacher's own performance. Most of the literature stems from the work of John Dewey. His ideas appealed to Sheila, who was able to refer to him as an authority when cynical colleagues attempted to dismiss her attempts at student-centeredness as a passing fashion.

Writing in 1899, almost 100 years before Sheila's struggle, in the context of a newly industrialized society that curiously prefigures our own technological society, Dewey challenged the ethic of individualism and the separation of mind from body and spirit (Dewey, 1899/1974a). Radically claiming that a school should be a community in which students help one another and work actively together on authentic tasks, Dewey also argued as early as 1904 for there to be time within the school day for both students and teachers to observe and to reflect (Dewey, 1904/1974b).

There is precedent for figuring out what it would take to translate Dewey's concepts of active learning, reflection, authenticity, community, caring, dialogue, and the whole child to a high school English classroom in the United States. Eliot Wigginton (1985) describes exactly that in *Sometimes a Shining Moment.* The cooperative learning literature assumes this kind of process and these effects (see the Resources on Student-Centered Teaching section at the end of this book). Carl Rogers (1951) devoted an entire chapter of his book, *Client-Centered Therapy,* to the relocation of his theory of person-centeredness to a classroom situation. He acknowledged the struggle of the counselor or teacher to stand back after establishing a safe relationship of "unconditional positive regard" and, by listening and encouraging learners to listen to one another, to allow the learners to "raise and shape the questions" (Adams, 1972; Freire, 1968; Rogers, 1977). In that process, learners construct their own knowledge.

The Need for Mentoring

The evidence of the data gathered for this study is that, according to Sheila, the support of the mentoring relationship was pivotal in allowing her to take risks in her classroom. The situation of a teacher who is new to a school system, whether or not he or she is new to teaching, is well understood to be fragile (Carey & Marsh, 1980; Floden & Clark, 1988; Locke, 1984; Nason, 1986; Sergiovanni & Starratt, 1979; Sharan, 1984; Zeichner, 1980). Clearly, however, there seems to be a particular need for the nurturing of student-centered teachers who are the ones most likely to be in conflict with prevailing norms (Britzman, 1985; Culley & Portuges, 1985; Freire & Shor, 1987; Goodlad, 1984, 1990). Despite efforts of teacher educators to present alternatives to traditional teaching in their university classes, the context of school culture is powerful. Like Sheila, even teachers who are already convinced that they want to and can operate student-centered classrooms face pressure to question their skills, and feel drawn to behave in ways that are consistent with the culture of the school (Rossman, Corbett, & Firestone, 1988; Sarason, 1982; Zeichner, 1980).

Reflection for Perspective

The literature on empowerment overwhelmingly supports the importance of students' talking through their understandings of texts and ideas in a situation in which they are clearly heard and respected. The literature on mentoring and teacher reflection consistently emphasizes the importance of emotional safety as the precondition for open exploration of ideas and feelings. Within the safety of an effective helping relationship, teachers can come to discoveries that significantly affect and change the quality of their teaching (Avila, Combs, & Purkey, 1973; Katz et al., 1974; Newman, 1980).

When teachers have the opportunity to dialogue in a sustained way, talking through their thoughts and feelings in the presence of a supportive, nonjudgmental listener, the opportunity to widen and perhaps even shift their perspective is created (Bussis, Chittenden, & Amarel, 1976; Gray & Gray, 1986; Kram, 1985; Munby, 1982; Wideen & Andrews, 1987). The experience of direct positive feedback may, more than anything else, create well-integrated, effective teachers by helping them feel positive enough about themselves to devote their time and energy "to the need satisfaction of others" (Combs, 1982, p. 162).

The job of the adviser, therefore, is to help the student teacher, beginning teacher, or in-service teacher move from supervision to self-vision (Dewey, 1904/1974a) through direct visits, in context, as an active presence in their classrooms, offering direct feedback to practicing teachers. Ideally, the adviser/mentor provides a mirror for the teacher, until the teacher has the confidence to look directly and honestly at him- or herself with acceptance as well as knowledge and clarity (Freire, 1968; Jersild, 1955; Joyce & Showers, 1983; Kohlberg & Mayer, 1972; Rich, 1990; Rogers, 1973).

Who should provide that advising? Fear of judgment interferes with the success of a teacher's being mentored by an administrator. Although the creation of mutual assistance among teachers is recommended as a safer alternative, research acknowledges what Sheila strongly felt within VCRHS: the fierce individualism and competitiveness to which we were all socialized in traditional schooling certainly persist among teachers, especially in high schools. Thus, the need exists for outside advisers to sustain teachers while they help them build community (Bussis et al., 1976; Katz et al., 1974; Sorcinelli, 1978).

Who would that be? The recently concluded 5-year study by Goodlad (1990) reinforces earlier calls for university support of student teachers beyond graduation (see also Joyce & Showers, 1983; Locke, 1984; Nason, 1986; Tabachnick & Zeichner, 1985). Goodlad's calls for "simultaneous renewal" of schools and teacher education openly advocate the frequent, consistent, active presence of teacher educators within the schools in rich, mutually respectful collaboration. His postulates form the basis for the hope that this book now represents—that the kind of relationship modeled here, or a variation on it, is a useful, fully possible, mutually beneficial, and absolutely necessary one for both teachers and teacher educators.

Notes

1. See the section at the end of this book for operational definitions of all terms.

2. All person and place names have been changed.

2 *Sheila's Vision*

Teacher as Nurturer:
Creating a Safe Environment for Growth

The development and articulation of Sheila's ideas and her efforts to translate those ideas into action as a teacher of high school English were represented in her choices, her interactions with students, and the students' interactions with texts and with one another. Before I actually observed her teaching at VCRHS, I recognized, from both the language in which she described what she was trying to do and the focus of her attention as she spoke, that this was a teacher who operated from assumptions about young people and about her work with them that were fundamentally different from traditional assumptions about students and teaching.

I chose to work intensively with Sheila because the more I saw of her teaching, the more I knew I could learn from her for my own teaching. She was already committed to student-centered teaching, and had figured out how to make it operate. All she needed from me was the perspective from which to allow her to believe in herself as I had come to believe in her.

Experiencing Empowerment Through Writing

To my knowledge, Sheila first experienced writing for empowerment in a graduate writing class in the school of education at the nearby university. It was as participants in that class in 1986 that she and I had first met and been interested in one another's ideas as expressed in shared reader-response papers and discussions. I had kept papers from that class, my own and copies of other people's, as a valuable text that had emerged from that experience of mutual empowerment.

In a reader response to Peter Elbow's (1981) *Writing With Power*, Sheila wrote that the process by which our class worked—sharing aloud and then responding to one another's reader-response papers—had helped her find her voice and hear it validated. She had already realized, from the process of the class as much as from the content, that her own previous writing had been judged rather than heard. She had been silenced by having to be guarded out of fear of a negative reaction, or no authentic reaction: "I write often for someone else's purposes. I write reports that are edited and added to other reports. I write papers that supposedly show the depth and breadth of my knowledge" (September, 1986).

What Sheila directly experienced in that graduate class was the safety within a classroom to share a kind of writing that could satisfy the self. As risky as she found it, writing out of her authentic thoughts and feelings became a risk that she was determined to take if, as a teacher, she was to ask students to take similar risks:

> I want to reach down inside of me to the feelings, to the real voice, and speak it and write it and experience its power and its magic, but I'm not quite sure how to do it or what it will sound like. . . . Maybe it won't even sound like me . . . maybe that's OK for a while.
>
> I know that I would like to see kids sharing and experiencing. . . . I know that I would like to be the kind of teacher that makes it safe to share, that says the right thing when the writing and reading are done. I guess more than saying the right thing, I want to say the real thing and use my real voice and be an example of theory in practice. (December, 1986)

In this kind of ungraded, unjudged personal response writing, and particularly in the listening, she and I found a new way to think about empowering our own students.

Thinking of teaching this way was very different from how she had thought originally in the troubled urban school that had been the site of her student teaching:

> The vast chasm between my students' public and private lives was something I did not even imagine, and I struggled to mold their public selves in my own image.
>
> I asked those children to leave whatever skills and abilities they brought from their homes and communities at the door, and become like me. I asked them to conform to a standard that simply contributed to the marginalization I sought to erase.
>
> I knew nothing of their alienation beyond the fact that they were not learning. Yet I blamed them. They were discipline problems. They were unruly. They didn't want to learn. They stood apart from me, and while I hated the distance, I did not know how to make it go away. The romantic notions quickly jaded and faded away.
>
> I understood for the first time that perspectives existed beyond my own and that student perception was a significant component in creating an environment where kids could learn.
>
> I believe that it is my job to continue to learn the ways of dialogue so that I can use language and, in turn, help my students to use language to reflect, criticize, rename, create, and change reality.

Her reader response to Paulo Freire's (1986) *Pedagogy of the Oppressed* prefigured the isolation she would feel 3 years later at VCRHS. She understood as oppression the fact that in schools people do not talk to one another, and committed herself to working against that oppression, at least in her own classrooms:

> So many barriers, both personal and institutional, inhibit and prohibit true dialogue. I am reminded of many schools where after the morning bell rings, doors shut and teachers never see each other, let alone talk to each other, for the rest of the day, or year for that matter.
>
> Who has a voice? Who doesn't? Who is listened to? Who is silenced? . . . If I do nothing else as a teacher, I must at least

encourage each child to find his or her voice and to join that voice with others to speak out for what is right and true. (November, 1986)

Vision of a Different Role

When I encountered her again 2 years later in the fall of 1988, Sheila had just returned to the university area to begin teaching at Valley Central Regional High School, one of the schools to which I was assigned as a supervisor of student teachers. In our earliest conversation that September, Sheila was feeling discouraged; her expectations for herself with her students were not being met. Confronting the dominant mode of teaching at VCRHS and the students' socialization to that mode, she felt isolated—even wrong—in her attempts to teach in the ways in which she believed. She was too embarrassed to have me observe her in her classroom.

She *would* talk about it, however. As we talked, Sheila was buoyed up by hearing her own instincts confirmed by the words of respected theorists, from beyond the narrow context of her particular school, as I reminded her of ones she knew—Dewey, Freire, Rogers, Tyler—and introduced her to others. Over time, she articulated with clarity and increasing conviction the kind of teacher she wanted to be:

- A nurturer of young people whom she deeply admires and respects
- An adult who models appropriate behavior
- A creator of a stimulating but safe environment for student growth
- A fully present human being within a community of learners

These convictions had been the basis for her prior experiments with student-centered teaching, and for her readiness to transform her own thinking even more fundamentally to implement strategies that would increase student-centeredness. The challenge of teaching by these convictions became Sheila's personal struggle for identity at VCRHS, as her beliefs and practices came into collision with the reality of most faculty's and students' traditional assumptions.

Although Sheila respected her own sophistication and range of experience as a reader and writer, she rejected the traditional role of teacher as owner and imparter of knowledge. She refused to see her role as being a judge of student performance. Nevertheless, she felt that her best skill was assessment. Assessment, as she spoke of it, meant sizing up situations, dynamics, and student readiness, and sensing when and how to intervene. She prized her ability to structure a lesson and a class session such that students would be working in ways that she had carefully predetermined that they should work, but she did not see her role as controlling student learning or student behavior. Rather, she preferred to think of herself as a facilitator, carefully designing situations so that students could move toward their own greatest possibilities.

For her and her students, she valued talk rather than silence, relationship rather than isolating individualism, and humor and pleasure rather than grim seriousness, all within the framework of intense, passionate, fully engaged, and connected work in consideration of ideas. Above all, she valued two things: her own and her students' authenticity, and their caring for one another.

The Struggle to Live the Vision

My observations of Sheila at work with her students confirmed that she was actually doing in her classrooms what she said she believed in doing, and living the role she described. Increasingly, as she developed a wider repertory of strategies for enhancing student-centeredness, and especially as she let go of center stage for both herself and the academic content, her vision became a reality for her and her students. As an unexpected result, to a great extent her vision became first a challenge and then a model for her colleagues.

When she finally allowed me to observe her teaching (November 22, 1988), it was immediately clear to me that, although Sheila had warned me that class was a "disaster," she nevertheless felt at ease in the classroom and genuinely respected and liked all of her students. In traditional terms, she was "in control" at all times: it was clear to an observer that the students fully accepted her authority. Her behaviors were those that nurtured their growth: comfortably walking among them as they worked individually; humorously defusing one boy's avoidance of the assigned task, letting him know that she liked him even if he had not done his homework; giving a lot of smiles and direct eye contact; touching shoulders or heads; listening with full attention to whomever was talking to her; and using ordinary language, frequently saying "good," "yes sir," and such personal appreciations as "you did a good job answering questions yesterday."

Inviting them to work together in pairs for the next task, she encouraged them to talk to one another. When some were reluctant to do so, she said, "Tell me." If two disagreed about an answer, she asked the parties to defend their positions to her first, modeling for them an active listening that she was urging them to practice. After the work in pairs, she declared each pair to be "experts" on their assigned section from the end of the book, *The Scarlet Letter* (Hawthorne, 1850/1981).

Their task was to present to the rest of the class what they had determined the meanings of certain difficult passages to be. Always, even when the speakers' voices were very soft, particularly in the large group now returned to desks in rows, students were listening to one another because they knew they would be held accountable for what the others had discovered. Occasionally Sheila reminded them, "It's OK to have different interpretations." Urged by her reassurance—"Don't let confusion stop you; talk from what you know"—students engaged in speculation that was thoughtfully based on details from the text. Just before the class ended, Sheila had them draw slips from an envelope to accompany a homework sheet:

> You will randomly receive one of the final chapters in the novel. Your assignment is to rewrite the chapter in your own words. Write this in the writing section of your notebook. Be prepared to discuss your version of the chapter with other members of the group, sharing your ideas and combining them to create a clear and entertaining version for the whole class. You will then be asked to read and explain your version to the class.

The students from this "disaster class" went out the door eagerly checking with one another to see with whom they would be working for the next week.

Three weeks later, I watched a different class share reader-response papers on Arthur Miller's (1953) *The Crucible*. The students were comfortable with one another, with Sheila, and with the sharing process. For most of the time spent listening to papers, they were respectfully attentive to whomever was reading or speaking. The language of the papers and the conversation were honest and direct, not inflated, raising questions that moved easily in and out between present day situations and the world of the Puritans on the surface of the play. In a brief, directed freewrite that followed the discussion, Sheila asked them to address whether "there are people in 1988 who are mistreated because they're different from 'the norm.' First decide what is 'the norm.' Is it completely unheard of that people are killed because they don't fit in?"

The peer editing that followed was done comfortably, with Sheila going around and encouraging students to use one another as resources (e.g., "Well, what does *she* think? You can trust her"). Most students remained on task the entire time, appearing to be confident that they were both heard and necessary in this process.

Balance. In mid-January of 1989, Sheila was struggling to figure out what to do herself while students were in cooperative groups. What *is* the role of a teacher in a student-centered classroom? In spite of the essentially nontraditional nature of her vision, the dominant model drew her. Her strong initial inclination was that she had to be part of each group: "Isn't it my job to *teach* them?" That inclination was in conflict with her stronger motivation to acknowledge and nurture the students' abilities to construct meaning with one another without direct instruction.

She worked hard to find a way to practice restraint without disappearing completely from the intellectual process. As I observed and she confirmed when we spoke after one class session (January 17, 1989), she was training herself to assess in each case how much latitude to give. Sometimes she intervened in a group that was off-task, offering guidance in the form of a time limit, a page reference, a clarifying question, or just support for the group members who were trying to stay focused. Sometimes she left a temporarily off-task group to itself as she eavesdropped from a respectful distance, accessible and aware of everything that was going on without interfering. The more she practiced that kind of active restraint, the more it seemed to suit her in terms of the kind of teacher she wanted to be.

Even when the content was fairly traditional, such as doing vocabulary or describing the different characteristics of transcendentalist versus romantic writing, her affect with the students showed intense attention to what they might be thinking, ready to adjust the process if it was not working: "I think we need to stop if people really don't know what we're looking for. Let's get a list, because you're confused and I'm confused."

Then, hearing one student's continued undercurrent of the question, "How do we pick all these things out of a poem?," Sheila readjusted again saying, "I think this is hard. There'll be *some* things." Then, she sent them back into partners "to pick out two or three of the list that you can find in the poem," giving a manageable task: "I'm going to ask each group for one verse to look closely at." As a result of this shift, students began to see connections between the academic content and their own teenage culture. The student who had asked the original question said, "I can find all these same things in a Judy Blume novel or in *Call of the Wild*" (London, 1914). Another student recognized aspects of romanticism in Guns 'n Roses songs. Two students argued over whether *Animal Farm* (Orwell, 1945) was romantic. The labels had become real for them in terms of what they already knew.

Empowerment as a New Agenda

In spite of what she had discovered in our graduate class at the university in 1986, it took 2 more years of teaching and then several months of intense reflection for her to see that her very success as a traditional teacher had been getting in the way of fulfilling her own high vision of student empowerment. She admitted that, in the past, she had never really thought about her expectations for her students, just her expectations for herself. Student-centeredness had not been her agenda:

> I put on a show. That's what I did. I was the entertainer, 'cause I do that. I know how to do it. Kids would say to me, "You're like watching TV." They would sit, and I would do it. I'd be jumping around and do this, do that. I entertained them, made a lot of jokes, was really funny.
>
> And I think there's a real fear, when you know that you can really captivate, to shut up, 'cause you don't know what will happen. It's a risk, to say, "What will happen if I shut up?"
>
> I think that what happens is that the kids that you least expect it [from] work. (June 16, 1989)

Sheila had begun her teaching of high school English in the traditional manner: teacher- and content-centered. Even then, however,
she had been different from most high school English teachers. Although she loved literature and was especially aware of the power
of language, her study of English had focused not on the traditional
canon but on such literature as the French existentialists. More important, her academic background had also included special education, guidance, and curriculum. Thus, it was not surprising that her
approach to the literature and writing content of her courses resisted
close examination of certain texts—knowledge *about* a text—as an
end in itself. Instead, she understood text to be a vehicle through
which students could consider certain issues of importance to their
own lives.

On those fundamental issues as Chapter 5 will describe in detail,
Sheila ran into conflict with her colleagues as a result of their different
priorities about content and different assumptions about their roles
as teachers. In spite of that conflict and the distress and doubts it
caused her, she never really lost sight of her larger goals: (a) to vali-
date students' lives exactly as they were and (b) to have them extend
their ability to appreciate the validity of other people's lives, thus
entertaining further possibilities for meaning in their own.

Now the work she wanted them to do would not satisfy her if it
was done merely for the teacher. Nevertheless, she was uncertain of
exactly how to design structures that would allow the work of the
classroom to offer students an understanding of themselves and the
world. As early as March 14, 1989, she stated this complex conviction:

> Sometimes I'm not sure why I want them to read. I want
> them as thinking people to have an experience of different
> philosophies so they can choose what they think. If every-
> thing is already decided, what good is it? I'm desperately
> afraid. If they're not willing to consider choices of ways of
> living . . .
>
> That's all I think teaching's about: offering choices. And
> literature is the place where I can most clearly teach it.

At the end of that month she said:

> If the kid doesn't like what he or she hears, he or she can
> choose. . . . You know, "I read Thoreau. I think he's a crack-

pot. I don't like what he has to say." But at least they have heard some other ideas besides one.

And I really think school is about confrontations all the time: confrontation and making people uncomfortable with their thinking so they're forced to have some new thoughts. I mean, I think every book is a confrontation in thinking. (March 31, 1989)

She knew that her perception of the function of literature was not commonly held by English teachers. By the time we were working together as adviser/researcher and teacher, she had carefully considered her own beliefs:

I think people want to be bound by their subject matter because it's safe and because then they don't get into trouble. But I think that if school is anything—and I've said this to you before—it's about teaching people how to be human. (March 31, 1989)

Sheila knew from her own experience as a reader what could happen from the kind of study of literature that she envisioned and was trying to put into practice, but she knew it came only from its being accessible to students. This is essentially what she had been saying a year earlier: "I think that if we simply talk about *Frankenstein* (Shelley, 1818/1984) but we don't make any connections to human nature—because all literature is about human nature—then it doesn't make any sense to me" (March, 1989).

She felt clear about this: that the teacher's job is not just to ask students to do what some high school English teachers call "lit crit"— that is, to become skilled at talking about a literature "out there," apart from themselves. Instead, "I think what happens to kids is they come, most kids, come to school with one view, and my impression of school always was you open up all of the possibilities" (March, 1989).

Sheila spoke of teaching as confrontation, but she did not mean conflict between student and teacher or between students and one another. She meant confrontation with ideas, often represented by characters living out their lives in worlds substantially different from the worlds that most of her students experienced. Dealing with those ideas involved careful attention to text, so that the characters and

their worlds could be understood as they were drawn. It meant that
students be clear about why they think the way they think, respecting
the integrity of the text rather than just asserting a position. Furthermore, especially because VCRHS was an all-white, essentially lower-
middle- and middle-class rural regional school, she felt an urgency
to have students question the context of their own comparative privilege:

> When you're dealing with kids you know will move into
> positions of power in the society, it's frightening to look at
> how they think, or how little they think, 'cause they will
> make decisions without ever considering what those deci-
> sions will mean for others. (March 28, 1989)

Here Sheila was thinking aloud about a heated argument in the
ninth-grade class I had just observed. Students had come up with the
issue themselves, from their previous small-group discussions. They
argued the question of which society in *Lord of the Flies* (Golding,
1954) was "better," Jack's or Ralph's. Her assessment of what she and
I had witnessed was that many of the ninth graders were still at the
stage at which they "simply wanted to hear themselves argue their
own point." But as she analyzed the classroom scene, her language
indicated that she felt sure that, within time and within the structures
she was creating, they would arrive at the next stages:

> They're not ready or they're not used to hearing someone
> else's point and discussing it, although as I watched a couple
> of pairs work together, they were really saying, "OK, now
> what did you say?"
> The other thing that was interesting is that people
> couldn't defend their positions. They were just loud, and
> that's why they complain, "Why do we have to use the text?"
> But they have to base their ideas on something and learn that
> you just can't make blanket statements.
> I'm saying to them that . . . just because they yelled the
> loudest or had the last word doesn't mean that it's true.

During that class, one student noticed that some of them were talking
about which society was "better," whereas others were talking about
which was "more appealing." Could Jack's violent solution be more

appealing because it meant survival, but still not be "better"? It was not lost on Sheila and me that the struggle to deal with that sophisticated moral issue was coming from the students themselves.

Accessibility:
Choosing Books That "Hook" Kids

For her teaching of adolescents, Sheila rejected the idea of a necessary canon of "great books" in favor of books that would "hook them in"—books that would engage students and challenge what they thought they knew. She would also use some conventional classics, but would start, she said, with something that students would really like, something that was immediately accessible to teenagers. First, she said, "They have to buy into wanting to talk about things that are hard" (January 1, 1990). Because she recognized that her students were at different places in their development, interests, abilities, and prior knowledge, she worked mostly from "choice books" as well as some books that the entire class would read. The choice books would allow individuals—hopefully in pairs so they could have conversations about their books—to decide what interested them and what they had to say.

One "anchor book" that she assigned to everyone, however, was Harper Lee's (1960) *To Kill a Mockingbird:*

> The kids loved the book. It was the most favorite book they read. They loved it because it really touches, I think, the basic issue for people and that is how you live a good life.
>
> What does it mean to be a good person? What is that going to mean for the decisions that you make, and how do you make those decisions? How far am I willing to go? (March 20, 1990)

Throughout the 2 years of our professional interactions, the character Atticus Finch from *To Kill a Mockingbird* was the hero to whom Sheila kept referring for the kind of modeling of courage, integrity, and empathy that she wanted students to see in both literature and life. Her aim for the teaching of that book was that readers would invest emotionally in the characters by reading and writing freely, by talking about it with other people, and by spending enough time in thought, writing, and talk to see that people have options in their lives.

Sheila was sure that the traditional ways of "studying" *To Kill a Mockingbird*—"getting" everything there was to get by full-class, round-robin reading, remembering of details, and quizzes—would not accomplish her aim, and might make students hate both the book and reading. Although she saw evidence all around her in the department that her approach to reading was not the norm, she felt strongly that focusing on how people make choices and on the consequences of those choices within the worlds of the stories would help readers live their own lives with more awareness, more sense of options, more imagination, and therefore more freedom.

Believing that the function of literature for high school students is neither escape nor distanced literary criticism, she had them read a range of works for a variety of reasons. One she chose was *I Am the Cheese*, a compelling book by Robert Cormier (1977) about a teenaged boy in search of his identity:

> 'Cause the kid *has* no identity. His identity has been changed. But what's more significant about it is that it really opens up for discussion why we believe what we do about America and in fact what might be true about America.
>
> People don't want to have that discussion. This is the most banned book in America. It's on top of the list. That's why I think everyone should read it. So, and then when we talk about why is it banned, what's bad about it? There's no sex, there's no violence, there's no swearing. Why is it banned?
>
> And they understand. They get it when they're done, although it's a hard book for kids to read. (March 20, 1990)

She did this because she felt that "learning comes not out of understanding," but it comes out of "being uncomfortable with something or needing to figure something out" (June 10, 1990). *I Am the Cheese*, she told me, "presents them with some ideas that they might not have considered before." Although Cormier's (1977, 1988) works may not be on the usual list of books required for high school students, Sheila liked him "because he portrays the way kids feel: he keys into their own ambivalences" (June 10, 1990).

On January 6, 1990, Sheila said of her long-range agenda, "My goal for them is really to come to some understanding that the things that we do in the world affect other people, whether we like it or not."

Sheila presented students with a wide range of engaging, accessible stories in which people who could be real make hard, real choices and live out the consequences of those choices. She required them to listen to points of view other than those they walked in with. She hoped to accomplish in one semester, one year, or even 3 or 4 years with a student the kind of education that Atticus Finch in *To Kill a Mockingbird* achieved over many years with his own children, Jem and Scout. She hoped to teach them that "you can't appreciate anyone until you, for a moment, try to imagine what their life is like":

> I think that in literature there's the opportunity to have a hero that's sort of average. Atticus Finch is an average guy. He was raising his family. He does something that's above average, but we would be called to that. We could be called to be ready to be above average when the need arises. (January 6, 1990)

3   The Process Is the Content

It was not just the content of the readings that asked Sheila's students to consider their own behavior in the world. Despite the pace and intensity of an English teacher's day in teaching a full load of classes, she consciously modeled respect for her students: welcoming them into the room in a manner that indicated she was genuinely glad to see each of them every day, hearing them with interest and taking them seriously, and dealing with their occasional disrespect to one another or her in ways that did not reproduce disrespect. Her tone of voice and clearly attentive body language conveyed to her students that whatever they thought, felt, said, or did, they were human beings whom Sheila valued. As time went on, I was able to observe students behaving with one another in many of those same ways.

The processes of the lessons Sheila constructed required students to develop respect for one another within the classroom. Although I was able to suggest certain strategies that she had not otherwise thought of, her use of them seemed to come naturally out of her expectation that all of her students were responsible, capable, thoughtful, intelligent, caring, and interesting human beings.

Whenever, as inevitably happens in a high school classroom, a student began a distracting cross-conversation within the large group, Sheila brought him or her back to the main focus in a way that respected the student as a person: "Steve, just stay with me so you'll be clear about what to bring tomorrow" or "Sean, it would be really helpful for me if everyone was listening." When students needed to interrupt our interviews during her lunch or other free time, she spoke to them in the same respectful tone of voice, honoring their needs as well as ours.

Sheila's reconceptualization of the role of a teacher had required her to call into question many of the teacher behaviors that often are institutionalized as "rules." For example, she chose to rethink for herself whether—and especially why—to ask students to raise their hands before speaking. She decided that the main thing was to make sure no one would be dominating the conversation while others were frustrated in their waiting to speak.

Teaching Is Not About Getting Your Own Needs Met

A more troubling issue for her was her own relationship with the students. At first, she said (March 31, 1989) that at VCRHS, she had felt more competitiveness, "more of an 'us-them' mentality," than she had felt in her previous teaching positions, and thus felt self-protective and wary of establishing intense closeness this time. Reflection brought the realization that she had been teaching as she had been taught, by the force of her own vibrant personality. As a performer, therefore, she had looked to her students to meet her personal need for validation. The process of talking through her vision helped her separate the students' needs from her own.

As Chapter 2 indicated, one of her initial expectations was that the students would like both her and her methods. That expectation was not immediately met at VCRHS. When we first began working together, she spoke of feeling alienated from these students, cautious and even a little afraid. Before we had concluded the study, however, she had worked through her initial distrust of the students. She realized that it was possible, necessary, and healthy to decide for herself what would be appropriate boundaries between genuine respect, caring, and affection for students on the one hand and her professional sense of self on the other. Her own clarity on that issue gave Sheila renewed energy for centering attention on their needs, abilities, struggles, and growth.

By June of 1990, Sheila felt she had achieved the balance toward which she had been working, between her own need to be involved and the students' development of responsibility:

> What's clearly different about the way I teach now than I used to teach is that I used to expect that my students would take care of certain needs that *I* have, or do or make me feel good about myself and what I do, and now I have no expectations for that at all.
>
> If they *do* it, that's great, but I don't look for it, I'm not waiting for it.
>
> I don't—I miss it sometimes, but I don't think in any way that they should be stroking me at all, and I used to really—I think I used to almost set it up so that they had to. I spent a lot of energy on that, like getting feedback, making sure that I was OK, making sure they thought I was a good teacher.
>
> Overall when I look at some of the interesting things that my students do, I think two things. I think they're pretty amazing and number two, I've learned that I can do better next time. And whether or not they like me or like the class or whatever is sort of a moot point. It's really irrelevant to what goes on in the room. (June, 1990)

Getting to that place took time. Once Sheila's relationship with the students fundamentally shifted, it was easier for her to let go of her fear of how other teachers would view what she did:

> And I'm sure that a lot of people perceive my class as very loose. Like there's a lot of freedom, and a lot of "kids can do whatever they want" type of attitude, even though I know and the kids know that is not the case. I think other teachers would perceive it that way.
>
> I think you have to give up ownership of the classroom. Once you do there's really nothing to be afraid of, because it's everyone working there together to make something happen, and sometimes it does and sometimes it doesn't, but it's not the end of the world. (June, 1990)

Learning From One Another

By the fall of 1989, Sheila and I seemed to be working together on the fine-tuning of facilitating a cooperative-learning situation. I commented after an early morning class on September 18 that when she was talking with small groups, her voice carried throughout the room. She said, "I'll practice with my voice in this class." She did, catching and correcting the level of her voice as she worked around the room.

At the beginning of that new school year of 1989-1990, Sheila was willing to live with the ambiguity of not knowing whether what she was trying would work. She was tampering with the most fundamental terms of school life—who talks in a classroom, where the chairs face, and whose ideas are considered to be important. It was not a comfortable position for her. What helped her feel more comfortable was reading a text on cooperative learning that I had recommended, *Learning Together and Alone* by David Johnson and Roger Johnson (1975). The reading reassured her:

> And they even said that structuring the difference between cooperative, competitive, and individual goals is really hard for teachers because we don't know how; we weren't taught.
>
> So then I felt better. I thought, "It's OK that I don't know how to do it, 'cause no one taught me."
>
> So I do feel that I have to keep reading and looking at the difference between what's a cooperative group and what are just like people in a group together. That's a problem for me.

It was a problem with which she was willing to struggle, because she was already fairly sure that this process embodied her vision of what should happen in school. She had just not known how to go about it by herself. But once she had begun, it was as if other rules were also open to question. Transforming the process of managing a classroom seemed to allow her, however tentatively at this point, to challenge the notion of a sacred body of knowledge:

> I think what I like about the individual reading of reader response is that I'm finding books. I'm learning about books

that kids really like, books that really hook kids in, that they can start and they finish all in one day because they can't put it down.

I think it opens the canon up. I know there's a literary canon, and I know there are books that are considered "great books." I'm not convinced they include all of the great books or all the great thinkers, and I think this class is just opening my literary canon to the possibility of using books that might not necessarily be considered. (September 10, 1989)

With all of the revolution in her thinking about and behavior within a classroom, however, Sheila had remained curiously unwilling to consider having the students move from their small groups into either a circle or a horseshoe for the full-class discussion. Many times I asked her about her insistence on having "home base" structured in rows. I commented that when the students were in rows, she had felt obliged to repeat a lot of what the students in the front were saying, and that those people in front seemed to talk out, unaware that people behind them had their hands up. She acknowledged that the behaviors I described were problems:

It's funny you said that because as I was standing there thinking this is a two-way conversation, I thought, oh, we shouldn't be doing it this way, but sometimes I'm not sure how something will go, so—I don't know, you know, I don't know how long it will take, you know, all those things, so I'm more hesitant. (September 10, 1989)

In that interview, we spent several minutes (four pages of typed transcript) in dialogue about the issue of rows as opposed to alternative constructions. At several points in the conversation, she seemed to be as ready to try this simple change as she had been to try the more radical ones I had suggested over the months we had been talking. She offered:

It would also get them in the habit of talking more to one another, which is a problem. I might still have to repeat, because some people are soft spoken, but not as much. That's true. Yeah. That's a good idea.

Nevertheless, desks in rows before and after small groups, that day and for the rest of the year, seemed to be the one embodiment of control and familiarity that Sheila needed to hang on to. Her reasons suggested that this was a blocked place for her. She claimed she needed to save time, even though she acknowledged that the transition from groups to a circle or horseshoe would take no longer than from groups to rows. She felt overwhelmed with the thought of moving back again to rows for the next class. She claimed rows facilitated her taking of attendance, but I noted that she didn't take attendance in most classes until she had given her instructions and the students were busily engaged in their groups, scattered all around the room. Rows, she finally admitted, were easier for her:

Sheila Plus I think it's easier if you have a substitute. All those things, like I have to give a seating chart for Ralph, and I just think that's easier.

Liz OK. And also it's better for the janitor. Janitors always prefer rows.

Sheila Well, at the end of the day I could always move them back like this. It's not like I couldn't *do* that. But it does facilitate certain things that I want to do, some of the time, not all of the time. (September 18, 1989)

What those "certain things" were became clearer on February 12, 1989. A class for whom working in groups was a new experience had gotten away from her, and she needed to pull them back: "I didn't like the feel of the room. The rows helped me control it, get it back to where I'm comfortable, which is what I was doing, and I felt it was good at the end."

She said to me in the late summer of 1990, "Furniture is important. You taught me that. Kids get the message. Some groups need that more than others. I like to *start* in rows, so *I* can set the guidelines."

What I came to realize over the many months that I watched Sheila teach was that (a) my own bias on the issue of furniture got in the way of my seeing, for a long time, that (b) after that September dialogue, Sheila seemed to have *solved* most of the problems that rows generally create for teaching. In every one of my field notes thereafter, my map of classroom interaction indicates that the conversation seemed widely spread around to include almost everyone present. People sometimes turned around to speak to one another, but even when they did not, I noted in class after class a real attitude of listening to one another that I had not thought possible within the physical structure that has people facing the backs of one another's heads. *I* needed to remember that the significant conversations happen in the small groups and that when people get interested in one another's ideas, the attention to one another can carry over into the large group no matter how the furniture is arranged.

At the end of August 1990, when I asked Sheila about what I referred to as her holding on to a remnant of traditional teaching, she reminded me of what I already knew—that even when the desks are in a circle or horseshoe, the class can be teacher centered. Even when the teacher is in the back of the room, she said, "If I engage, they turn around and talk to me." Surface appearances are not guarantees.

She was therefore very much "in control" of the classes that she taught. Unlike a traditional teacher, however, she was asking that her students pay attention to their own thinking, to one another, and to the texts in front of them, as well as to her instructions. The control, the careful planning and organizing, and the attention to dynamics of space and relationships as well as of time and text existed for the sake of creating an environment in which students could find their own power.

What Teaching Is About

As she got used to the student-centered strategies, they became a vocabulary that fitted her agenda of empowerment. As I watched her classes operate, even when the seating returned from small groups to conventional rows, the large-group conversations that followed small group decision-making were lively, mutually attentive and respectful, and inclusive of almost everyone. Sheila was sure that to a great extent this full participation represented people's safely reporting or further developing of ideas that they had already tried out on a smaller number of peers. In fact, frequently, especially in her course titled "I'm Nobody. Who Are You?" (which she told me had drawn many students whose self-esteem was shaky), she validated effort and achievement on the spot. As she went around to groups, eavesdropping and quickly checking in on and extending progress,

Sheila invited people to prepare to repeat to the entire class "when we get back together" what they had just been saying to one another.

As they spoke in the large group, she recorded student insights on the board, "keeping track of all the information we came up with together." When all the separate decisions appeared before them, they could see that they had, with one another and without direct instruction, generated the important things that needed to be said about a reading. Her closure of such a lesson was always as much affective as academic. Along with the assignment to go on reading and writing—bearing in mind what they had just come up with in class—and to "find all the examples so you can tell me what you know and how you know," she told them, "You did a really great job today! I'm really impressed!"

The task in her classes was for students to "make meaning" with one another about what they were reading, rather than trying to ingest what a teacher or other authority had decided the meaning should be. For a book as confusing as *Fade* (Cormier, 1988) or *I Am the Cheese* (Cormier, 1977), Sheila acknowledged the difficulty of "knowing" and reassured them that they would be able to handle the task:

> Make a list of everything new that you and your partner can put together about the character, with the page numbers. . . . All the little things will turn out to be important, and they'll help it not seem stupid. If you're confused, write down what the question is. . . . If the two of you have differing reactions, write down both.
>
> It's OK for you to be confused—you're interpreting based on what you know. (March 22, 1990)

By the end of the semester, one of the nonreaders in that "I'm Nobody" class had read 23 books! Sheila was proud of her but not surprised, because as early as mid-February she knew the process was working, even with—or maybe especially with—those particular students: "If the goal is engagement in literature, if the goal is critical thinking, if the goal is considering new ideas—if these are the goals for an English teacher, I meet those goals."

Her view of what was important to teach was consistently at odds with the judgments usually made in traditional schooling. She felt that the traditional teaching of English, by its distancing from

students' lives, does a disservice to students, especially to young
men:

> I'm leaning toward trying to figure out how young men are
> encouraged in a school system to reconcile the dichotomy of
> being male in our culture, which is to be loving and sensitive
> and caring and at the same time retain masculinity.
>
> Because I really think school does not encourage people
> to feel, to have feelings, to respond to things at a gut level.

Not that, for Sheila, the gut level of response was enough. As she told
me on March 5, 1990, "Your gut feelings are sometimes affected by
things that are inaccurate, and we need to get closer to what's true,
not just what we feel, although that's where we start."

But traditional English teaching, she felt, forgets the starting
place:

> I think that's something that bothers me about [literary]
> analysis. Analysis is very distant. You look as the critic at
> something. You don't look at it as yourself, as feeling, as
> emotion. I think that's really lacking.
>
> I think that's what's hard about history. I think why kids
> say they don't like history is because they cannot make the
> connections to themselves. . . . That's why one of the things
> I do with American literature, I'll say, "Take on the voice now.
> Write in the voice. You are the person."
>
> That really makes things personal for the kids and then
> it makes sense. (February 12, 1990)

The affirmation of her agenda was in the students' understanding of
it. On March 5, 1990, one of the students I interviewed said, as the
others nodded agreement, "She wants you to think. She wants you
to be able to defend your position and make your point, to make her
actually believe what you have to say. That's basically what she
focuses on."

The Stove Isn't On

The students told me that Sheila was interested in what *they*
thought, not in whether they could reproduce what she or any other

so-called "authority" thought (March 5, 1990). It had taken them a while to realize that she really meant that and would operate on it. Jessie, the valedictorian, told me on April 27, 1990,

> Before I had her, I never really—I didn't think anyone really cared what I thought. . . . She actually has us write essays in first person, just what *we* thought, and I thought it was pretty neat that anyone would actually *care* what I thought about. It was just so nice having someone, knowing that someone actually listened to you.

Sheila spoke frequently about her determination to make her classroom a safe space for students to take risks with ideas, feelings, and language. She worked hard to create that kind of space, in which no one got hurt, humiliated, or left out. On April 27, 1990, Sheila described what she had learned about students' hesitation to let go of fear:

> I think Nicole really said it well: that whole idea that what is most important is your own understanding. And I think that's what I'm really trying to get them to believe—'cause they've been taught that that isn't true.
>
> By the time they get to ninth grade—probably by the time they're in third grade—they already know that what they think is not important at all, and they need to shut up. So they're waiting, and they're so fearful.
>
> The thing that kills me about kids is that they know what it's like to be wrong, and they know what it's like to be humiliated. It's kind of like you touch the hot stove one time, and that's the only time you touch it. They're not fools. They've learned. Why suffer?
>
> But what I try to show them in my class is that the stove isn't on. . . . It's OK.

She worked behind the scenes, essentially, to create that safe space. She sought out students in their study halls if they had not gotten their work in or were confused or unprepared, and she sat with them as they worked on it: "I worry a lot about the kids that aren't necessarily getting it, especially the special ed kids that come into the class and are struggling" (December 1, 1989).

Sheila also did that for any student who was not performing, for any reason. She encouraged drafts and rewrites until the student was satisfied with a paper; called parents to tell them about the good things their children were doing; baked cookies for the class, and sometimes sent cards or gave small presents such as bookmarks; knew individual preferences in music; she praised and hounded. She worried about students who were outcasts or were tormented or misunderstood by teachers or peers. She would not allow aggressive students to shout down shy students.

Students knew that Sheila cared about them. Moreover, Sheila believed that a teacher should care in the way that she cared. Thus, it was devastating to her to realize that her behaving, as Ralph said "like a mother" with her students, was not respected by other faculty members. However, in spite of what she heard and felt to be the disapproval of many of her peers, and the academic distance that she saw to be the norm to which she felt she was supposed to conform, Sheila persisted in her conviction:

> I really feel like these parents lend me their children. I have them in my room for 45 minutes a day. They're in my care. I have to treat them with care. I don't think of myself as an academician who's imparting knowledge. I don't feel that way about high school. (December 1, 1989)

If faculty members did not value Sheila's "mothering," her students did. I heard this from more than one of them:

> If you need help or something she's not somebody you're afraid to ask. Some teachers are intimidating . . . you just hesitate, and she doesn't make you feel like—if you don't understand or something like that, she—you know, it's OK. (December 18, 1989)

One of Sheila's earliest concerns was about her own self-protective distancing from the students when she first came to VCRHS, in reaction to what she perceived to be student-closedness. Why were these students closed? Her analysis was that a high school is not set up to attend to feelings, which creates problems on many levels. Frequently, especially during the spring and summer of 1989,

Sheila expressed frustration that the structure of that school, as well as other public schools she had been in, did not allow the time or the situation for students, especially boys, to process difficult feelings. For example, after a speaker came to talk about AIDS in mid-May of 1989, Sheila kept wondering where young people could go with the deep feelings that such events necessarily draw forth:

> What was incredible to me was there was no time when it was over for kids to just hang out and talk. I met up with C.J. to go over—he was like trying to do an assignment. He talked for 45 minutes about this man. He was almost in tears. He felt really sad.
>
> He had a lot of conflicting emotions, and I thought, why aren't we letting kids just talk about the things that they're really worried about? They're really worried about AIDS. They have a lot of issues about sexuality. We're telling them about it. We're not letting them tell us. So I just sat there and listened, and he just went on and on. I don't really know what he said. He just had so many things in his head about meeting this man. He said he was really worried that people would be mean to him.
>
> I thought to myself, this is what kids need. They need more confrontation with things they're afraid of or unsure of. . . . I mean I think he could have cried, and there's no place. There's no time in the day for that. (May 9, 1989)

Traditionally, teachers play it safe, she mourned: "Even the adults don't want to ask the real questions" (June 16, 1989). Speaking of herself, Sheila frequently commented that she was probably considered crazy—"wacko"—because she was one teacher who felt that the classroom should be a place for strong feelings. She herself would cry openly during the films she showed in her class. Students knew that she cared passionately about many of the issues raised in the literature and about many issues from the world outside the classroom. Likewise, she invited students to be as personal and as passionate in their reader-response journals as they needed to be. She was convinced that in their engagement with (rather than academic distance from) pieces of literature, they would discover options for their own lives.

Apart from expecting herself and wanting her colleagues to behave in ways that would not undermine students' respect for themselves and one another, Sheila wanted them honestly and courageously to address serious and sometimes uncomfortable issues:

> I really worry because I think schools are really not talking to kids. People in schools, we're not talking to each other about the things that are really important. . . . I just think that things are not engaged in anything beyond the superficial level. (December 1, 1989)

She especially hoped that the male teachers would talk to the boys in the building about appropriate ways of expressing feelings, helping them see that males could have strong feelings other than anger and still be acceptable in society:

> I talked a lot about boys laughing about things that were violent in the video. Most of the people said things like, "that's boys."
>
> I said, "When you laugh, you sanction it for young men."
>
> The men said, "The boys are insecure." I said, "That makes it more important for you not to make jokes." (December 13, 1989)

She worried deeply about denial of real feelings:

> What is so true about young men in schools is that they have these internal conflicts between being what they think they're supposed to be, and being pulled in other directions. . . . How can you be both? How can you be compassionate and loving and a macho man? How do you reconcile it? And for women, on the other hand, how can you be assertive and strong, and loving? (January 26, 1990)

Student Centered:
The Focus Is on the Students, Not the Teacher

Knowing that she was a "good person" did not mean that Sheila felt she was always right or that she never made mistakes. Indeed, she was very hard on herself about perceived as well as actual mistakes, as later sections will show. What she did know was that she was willing to admit that she made mistakes as she tried to "figure out what the best way is for the students, not what the best way is for me" (December 1, 1989):

> I think you have to put your ego aside when you're in the room with kids, because there are too many egos that are bumping into each other. And it's funny. I'm not a very secure person, but when I'm in a classroom my ego's not a consideration for me. (January 7, 1990)

Her commitment to focusing on the students' needs rather than on her own or on the requirements of an academic schedule was consistent with the fundamental approach that allows for successful heterogeneous grouping. This approach was described to me by Ernest, the principal of VCRHS, when we spoke: "The primary thing is that the thrust of it (heterogeneous grouping) came from teachers putting kids first. And I think that makes all the difference" (February 12, 1990).

Putting kids first seemed to be a given for Sheila. What it meant to her was, for one thing, that she was not trapped in an adversarial relationship between her agenda and theirs, simply because as she saw it the learning she wanted to happen was contained in the process of a session as much as in its content. She managed the class by tuning in to what they were about as individuals and as a group.

In our first formal interview (March 31, 1990), she sorted out variables of response and tone from a class I had just observed: "I want them to get through the task, but I'm also paying attention to the way they go about the task."

Her job as teacher, she felt, was primarily that of intense, active paying attention to what was going on, which was expressed in the alert, leaning, fully concentrating affect of her body as much as in the decisions she made within a class period. She was listening for tone, as well as on-task behavior, respect for one another, and clarity of ideas. When things did not go as she had expected, she characterized the class experience in language that a mother might use about her children and about her own adjusting of plans to meet their needs as she read them:

What I've noticed is that they get together in a group and they're fussy. . . . So I don't know, I don't know. Maybe they're tired. We've been doing the stories for about a week and a half. Maybe we've done enough. Maybe we should stop. (May 9, 1989)

Her ongoing work of designing curriculum came out of the events of the classroom as the intellectual and affective needs got defined. Even though she had worked all summer choosing books and thinking about lessons, what she ultimately decided to do tomorrow came out of what happened in the classroom today. Taking the students into account was a loving kind of attention, understanding where they were coming from in order to help them grow:

Most kids want you to like them, and they want it to be easy. They don't want to feel like it's really hard and you don't like them.

I think we have to remember what it's like to be 14, 15. You get terrible things. You come to school [with] zits on your face and you think you're the ugliest person in the world. There is such beauty in that to me. (July 10, 1989)

Continuing to reflect during the summer of 1989, Sheila expressed her commitment almost as a statement for beginning teachers:

I've made a lot of mistakes. When I should have shut up I said too much. When I shut up I should have said something. That's the beauty of it. I think that's the beauty of the job. You learn as you go.

And kids are very forgiving. It's great. What you'd probably get fired for in a business, kids forgive you for, unless it's a really bad mistake. I've been fortunate. I haven't made too many bad ones.

You have to be a watcher. I think in teaching the one thing you have to have is an instinct. I think you have to know how to read people. If you're not good at that, that's going to be hard, because I think you have to be able to read the crowd, like tune in.

That will be the only thing I think you have to have some clue about. The rest you have to learn.

Responsibility

In November of 1989, Sheila gave credit to a previous year's class for their patience with her as she explored with them the possibilities of open-ended reader response and less formal teacher direction. Feeling responsible to that class for their having allowed her to experiment with greater student-centeredness, she saw their inexperience with certain traditional skills as her own failure. The students felt differently. Several of them told me in mid-December of that year that they appreciated, above all, her caring about them and about what mattered to them, and her letting them work out their own ideas. The students appreciated that she really read whatever they wrote in their journals and wrote them something back, so they didn't feel "like you're just writing to no one" (March 5, 1990). Over and over, students reaffirmed that what counted for them, which they were experiencing with Sheila, was the personal contact. The ways she achieved it varied. In that same interview (March 5, 1990), one boy told me, "She really gets around to see us. She makes a point of that every single day." In terms of work, at any given point she knew exactly where everyone was in their writing, because she had read their drafts and watched their progress; she knew where they were in their reading because she kept up with their daily reader-response journals. If individual students decided they did not want to finish a certain book, Sheila would ask them to write in their notebooks, "I stopped here because . . ."

Believing in the importance of process over product, she would not let large projects get to a final stage and be ready for evaluation before she saw them, especially if the projects were collaborative. Her aim was students' success, not her judgment. Therefore, she made sure, even from a respectful distance, that students were either participating fully or else talking to one another about why, and about how to work together better.

With individual students, it was clear from the beginning that she was unwilling to write anyone off. Other teachers may have been annoyed with Dave's unwillingness to take any step without asking, "What are we supposed to do?" Sheila, without impatience, would say to me, "That's Dave. That's the way he is." Because she genuinely enjoyed him, she found ways to encourage him to value his own initiatives but also to be aware of the needs and rights of others. When a student behaved inappropriately, she would intervene immediately in ways that gave the offender clear choices in terms of her insistence that all people be shown respect but without loss of her affection:

> The 10th graders—I mean, it's kind of funny. It's funny because I just want to be really careful about how I deal with them because I don't want to say, "You're a jerk; shut up." On the other hand they are jerks and I want them to shut up so I have to figure out what is appropriate. So I try to have a sense of humor and laugh with them as best I can. (March 20, 1990)

The students' reports to me about these infrequent run-ins were that Sheila was always fair and never insulting, and that she guided students through the process of learning the social skills they knew they would need.

It seemed to me that the students understood her perspective in these situations because from the beginning they were the focus of all of her decisions. As early as March 31, 1989, she told me about how she worked at getting groups to discuss rather than just copy one another's information:

> I tape-recorded them. One day I taped all of them, because I realized that they were not discussing; they were listing, except for Kelly's group. I wanted them to hear the difference: "Here's someone listing information and everyone else just saying, 'OK, I'm writing it down.' Here's a group saying, 'Well, why did you think that?' and 'Where did you find that?' "
>
> And it was great. For that moment they heard the difference.

That activity was successful. But at the beginning of our working together, she was struggling with the problems that can arise when a teacher relinquishes control of the classroom: "Kids who are insecure either dominate or they simply copy. I feel like I need to give them a third choice, but I'm not sure what the third choice is" (March 31, 1989).

In the November 1989 interview she looked at the problem in another way:

And quieter kids—that's why a small group works to their advantage, because those kids get a chance to talk, to speak. So I think that might be the next step, is having them work together, brainstorming a list, getting it up on the board, everyone looking at those ideas, seeing things that maybe *they* didn't see that they think might be important.

Maybe that's a way to go. That way they're working together, they're getting a lot of different perspectives.

A few months later, she was still figuring out how to get students to internalize their own responsibility: "I *can* grade them. I can say, 'I will grade how well the groups listen to each other.' That's a motivator. I hate doing that, but I can do it. For 10th grade, it might be a good structure for them" (February 12, 1990).

By the time the students talked with me again (March 5, 1990), Sheila seemed to have successfully solved the perennial cooperative-learning problem of individual accountability. Students understood that their reader-response journals and her eavesdropping kept them and their peers from hitchhiking:

She knows what each person has done. . . . When we're working in a group, she'll go around and talk to us, people in the groups. We won't know it but she'll be behind you listening, so she'll hear who's there and who's doing what. And in other classes they just say, "OK, it's group time," and they'll sit and do their own work and they won't be intertwined with the groups.

These interactions worked because Sheila's preparation for them was by no means purely academic. The students were her text: "You know, there are some days I can't wait to get there. I just can't wait. Not for the adults—I could care less if *they* all went away—but I think [the students] have *so* much to offer me."

As later chapters will show, Sheila's enthusiasm for what her students had to offer *her* became transformed into what seemed to both of us to be an even healthier relationship with them. Still adoring their passion and their brilliance and still and even more intensely challenging their detractors, she gradually separated her own need for affirmation from their successes. Practicing strategies for gradually disengaging herself from their struggles, she was deeply satisfied with facilitating their coming to know and appreciate themselves and one another.

Admiring and Respecting Young People: Believing That "Kids Can Do It"

Sheila's vision of the role of the teacher as both participant in and facilitator of the learning process of people she deeply admired and respected was a developing one over the course of the study. Before we started working together, she already admired high school students for being basically "interesting people," especially because they were ardent, open, alive, and basically unjaded. The hardest thing for her to believe fully was that she could trust them to generate, without her intercession through leading questions, meaningful interpretations of what they were reading. In spite of her not having recently read either Freire or Dewey nor much of the other literature on student empowerment (Adams & Horton, 1975; Bussis et al., 1976; Combs, 1982; Freire, 1968; Rogers, 1977), however, Sheila's regular personal experience of watching and hearing her students and finding them brilliant helped her take the risk of trusting that they could construct their own knowledge.

At first, especially between March and May of 1989, she vacillated between her joy—"They're fantastic!" or "They got it all by themselves!" or "It was beautiful!"—and her doubts—"Can they?" or "Should I?" or "Will they?" In April 1989, she described a video made by two students to represent their understanding of the transcendentalists:

It started out with U2 singing, "But I still haven't found what I'm looking for," and it was Emerson. One of the kids was Emerson. What a great song to pick for Emerson. He assumed this persona and this accent, and he talked about himself.

Then he sort of went to Jimi Hendrix, and this kid dressed as a hippie. This kid's like making connections to his way of thinking to Emerson, and then they met at the end. It was like 20 minutes long. It was great. At the end they said, "Did you get why we played the U2 music? Did you make the connections?"

It was great. It was better than anything I could have said about Emerson.

This semester the kids have done some really interesting things, and I think that I'm being influenced to take more risks.

By the end of the summer of 1989 and especially by the middle of the next fall semester, Sheila was beginning to trust that if a teacher knows her students well and believes in them, they can meet her realistic expectations. She had watched their success with taking on personae in writing and in acting. She found their energy, their inventiveness, and their resourcefulness wonderful. But she still had to work on herself when the activity seemed, on the surface, to be more like the traditional reading, writing, and discussing. On September 10, 1990, she acknowledged, "I intervene too much. I keep jumping in. I have to *believe* they can do this."

Having another teacher present who was conscious of and trying himself to practice student-centeredness may have helped. Her department chair, Ralph, talked to me about having witnessed her desire to have the students come up with their own thinking and her tendency to jump in. Regarding the class they were team-teaching, he said on September 18, 1990,

It's a learning process for both the teacher and the student and it's very difficult. I know Sheila works with me and there are several times when I say to her, "You've got to be quiet" and it's difficult.

And now when she goes to do something she'll say to me, "Should I say it?" and I'll say, "No!" and then when it's finished she'll say, "Oh! Everything I expected to happen

happened!" or "They answered all the questions I was going
to ask them!" which is exactly what we wanted.

At the very beginning of their collaboration, she and Ralph were
practicing this dynamic together. Inspired by Sheila, Ralph said,
"They are capable of getting there if we give them time to get there."
He went on:

> I think she made a good pitch to the class the other day,
> because she was going to ask them some information and
> give them some information, and then suddenly she turned
> to me and said, "Should I give it to them?" and I said, "No.
> Go ahead and see where they go."
>   And by the end of the class she said to them, "You know,
> I was worried you couldn't get there, and you got there! You
> brought out all the points that I was going to make!" And for
> the class that was an important boost, because it made them
> think, "Ah! We can do it by ourselves."

What made the difference between Sheila and Ralph that semester was that the range of literary interpretations Sheila was willing to
accept from the students gave them greater latitude than Ralph was
ready, at that point, to accept. In Sheila's perception, Ralph and the
other English teachers had some clear ideas about what needed to be
said about certain pieces of literature. Sheila, instead, was willing to
be stunned by how the students read:

> It's fantastic. They're really smart. I notice that all the time
> when I say to them, "What do you think?" and they start
> really thinking about what they think. They have great ideas.
>   I don't necessarily agree with them, or that isn't neces-
> sarily how I'd interpret it, but it's just as valid the way they're
> seeing it. (September 18, 1989)

She understood the risk she was taking: "It's power, and control,
and it's fear: What if you can't control what they come up with?"
(September 10, 1989).
    What if, indeed? Her instinct was to take the next step of trust-
ing the students, moving through her own fear. Struggling in mid-
October against her own feeling that she should be following Ralph's

more traditional agenda, Sheila also knew, "I feel like at some point, yes, I want them to know what a plot is. I want them to know those things, but a lot of these things they will discover on their own."

In that same interview (October 16, 1990), she defended the reader-response journal that she believed in as "their starting point to engaging with their book":

> It's a place to keep track of references, important things that happen in the story, but it is also the place where they say, "I like the book," "I don't like the book," "This is what I think so far," "Why did this happen or why did that happen?" or "This really is exciting me."
>
> That's where *they* say what they think, because in a formal paper they don't get the opportunity to do that. So if they don't get to do it somewhere, they're not doing it. They're not responding at all to the book on their own level.

After less than 2 months of using the reader-response journals, Sheila was thrilled to see that most of her students had begun to move from summary to analysis, without her having to call it that. By November 13, 1989, she was sure of the process: "They will make all the important points, I'm convinced of it, but they have to hear each other and they have to keep track of it."

Three months later, she reaffirmed that students *can* do this work: "They found all the important things about the book. They can *do* that, but they have to be willing to listen to each other" (February 12, 1990).

But their first job was to learn to listen to themselves. When a new 10-week quarter started in April of 1990, Sheila felt confronted again with a class she considered difficult. The composition of this one was similar to that of her original "disaster" class of November, 1988—predominantly boys, several of whom seemed too large or too preoccupied for schoolroom desks that somehow were terribly uncomfortable for them. For the session I observed, on April 27, the homework assignment had been to read Eudora Welty's (1982) short story, "The Worn Path." They were to notice language and to underline on their photocopied version the details that they liked. Some students also had written comments in the margins, which Sheila encouraged.

The first task of the class period was a brief initial response to the story. Sheila asked for five sentences: "Push yourself to write." Then she got them into partners to share these responses and then, first, to "decide together on five details you like and why" and second, to "look at what dialogue explains or reveals." Almost everyone wrote and almost everyone talked, some quite animatedly, trying to figure out what it meant that the character was named Phoenix, what really happened and why, and why her eyes were blue.

When they came out of groups, Sheila validated all readings of the story, encouraging them to speculate but to back up why they thought what they thought, allowing them to be different readers of the same story. By the end of the class, which had started at a very low energy, my impression was that everyone was listening to one another and was even excited about what details might suggest:

Darrell This may be her trail of tears!
Ned Ooooo! . . . Maybe she didn't get to the doctor on time, and she's trying to make up for it?

Sheila, herself energized by the quality of their insights, ended the class with a challenge: "Be able to say on Monday what you think has happened."

What I observed in that class reinforced what Sheila consistently told me about how she saw her role of guiding her students not to so-called right answers but through processes that would enable them to do careful reading of texts and real listening to one another. This happened for students partly because she herself modeled it, and they felt heard.

Sheila was able to tell me in each postobservation interview why she had made the decisions she had made about who would work with whom and why, and when to intervene and when not to and why. Her reasons always had to do with what she understood each individual student needed at that particular time: "Josh and Matt really struggle, and Mark would tell them everything, how to think and what to know. I want Josh and Matt to struggle. They feel comfortable enough with each other" (March 20, 1990).

Her aim seemed to be realized. Comfortable now with one another, with texts, and with their own perceptions, Sheila's students seemed more able to take the risks in their thinking that allowed them to amaze her and one another with their insights. The basis on which she chose to operate showed that she was comfortable with that level of risk-taking:

> Now I'm not saying I don't go into the classroom with more knowledge and skills than my students have. I'll admit to that. But what I think is that when we start something together, it's discovery.
>
> When I ask them for more information it's 'cause I'm learning. I want to know more about that because I never thought about that before, and maybe they'll change the way that I thought about something.
>
> I mean even if it's facts . . . you can have a fact but you can respond to the fact in a lot of different ways. It's not like there's only one way. (March 20, 1990)

Expecting amazing insights from her students was normal for Sheila. Her vision of what was natural and to be expected was not, however, the norm of teacher thinking. Ralph, who also was trying to restructure his classes toward student-centeredness, was more restrained than was Sheila about what students could do when you let them:

> Often what happens is, well, not often but a few times, their own perception of what we've given them or what we asked them to do is quite different from what our perception is, and sometimes their perception is better than ours, so we go with theirs (laugh). (January 26, 1990)

But Sheila had no such reluctance about going with what the students generated. In the classroom, she made it her role to record on the board when students reported their discoveries and then invite them to see the patterns they had generated:

> Sometimes I do things really right, so when kids are done they think, "Wow, I really did this. This is great. I get something."
>
> I sort of mapped out what it is they were saying . . . , and they looked at it and they looked at me and said, "Did you plan for this to happen?"

I said, "Absolutely not. It was brilliant. If I had planned
it it couldn't have worked out this beautifully. It just
wouldn't have happened." (November 10, 1989)

Ultimately, Sheila understood, it was her believing in them that
gave her students the freedom to create in the way she had consistently observed them to be doing, and to come to believe in themselves in the process. On April 22, 1990, she said to me, "If you limit
them then they're limited; but if you don't, they're not. It's so simple."
On April 27, she said of students who don't yet participate, "I think
they've just been trained to be passive, and that's what they do." With
that analysis, she was ready to recommit herself to working harder
with them, right then and the next year, to help them feel their own
power.

4 Teaching in a Student-Centered Classroom

Sheila was willing to do a tremendous amount of work to accomplish her agenda of student empowerment. Occasionally she resented it, therefore, when she saw colleagues doing what seemed to be much less work, following commercially prepared lessons. She was especially resentful when some of those teachers teased her, saying that she did not seem to be working as she walked around the building checking study halls for her students. However, she came to accept both why she had to do things her way and why other teachers did what they did:

> The incredible pace I described is why a lot of teachers give worksheets or have the kids answer questions at the end of the chapter: because they run out of steam.
>
> It's really hard. Sometimes when I go home, I feel really angry that I spend 3 hours designing my own activities, figuring out how I can make something go better.
>
> But I've made a commitment to myself this semester to design my own activities, because I think they're better than anything else I'm going to find. (January 26, 1990)

Thinking about her own commitment provided a framework for making choices about student accountability. In that same interview, she spoke to a question that skeptics of student-centered processes invariably ask: Can they get by in here without doing the work?

> It would be hard. I'd know from their notebooks. But without a test or a worksheet—you can *do* all those things, but you don't *have* to. They're not the only way to make sure kids are reading, in my opinion.
>
> It's a lot of work, but it pays off when they do good work. They're engaged, and it's not just . . . spitting back information. (January 26, 1990)

In fact, Sheila's vision had nothing to do with the acquisition of information. On April 27, 1990, she spoke with more emotion than at any other time about what she wanted for her students. What she wanted was already happening, she said with great joy, for some of them:

> I think that's what teaching is. It's like saying, "It's OK to come closer."
>
> That's what Darrell is doing. He's getting closer and closer to himself. That process is happening for him, and that's the success of teaching. *He* is doing it.
>
> I mean he was ready to do it. He came ready, but—and even Scott is writing poems that would blow your socks off. He's ready to do it and he's willing to take the risk and say, "I'm going to put myself out. Here I am for the world to see. I'm going to take the risk."

The Issue of Talk

Sheila recognized her own inclination to jump in and fill up silence in a classroom with her own talk. Her reconceptualization of her role had caused her to question what was traditionally called good teaching. Responding to an example in Theodore Sizer's (1984) *Horace's Compromise,* Sheila said:

I'm not convinced Sister Michael is a good teacher. She stands in front of the room and the class centers around her. If she is not there what happens? Can the class function on its own? Would the discussion be as lively and engaging?

I don't agree that teaching is like acting. That implies, once again, that the teacher should be on stage, the center of attention. (September, 1989)

Sheila could criticize the role because she had performed it:

I know . . . that in my early years of teaching I loved to be the center of attention. I laughed, told jokes. The kids loved me. I was like watching TV. They were just sitting, watching me. I did all the work. I put on a good performance. What did they do?

Changing my view of teaching has been a slow process for me. I have had to struggle with the issue of silence Sizer talks about. When the room got quiet, I thought nothing was happening. I would fill it up—Blah-Blah-Blah!!!

Now I know that silence is where ideas are born and the courage to speak is gathered. When I am quiet, my students speak and they are brilliant. (September, 1989)

She described the contradiction she felt:

Letting them struggle made me uncomfortable. I thought my job was to help them and make it easier. But thinking for them or giving them the answers didn't help them learn. It only taught them that they didn't have to think because I'd think for them. (September, 1989)

The consequence of teacher talk was student passivity, which troubled Sheila. Deciding to restrain the dominance of her own voice came from her commitment to let the students find theirs. At the same time, she began to risk trusting students to arrive at what they needed to get from a text, without her direct intervention.

Having committed herself to such a vision for change, Sheila began to see ever more clearly the extent to which she was different from other teachers, even people she respected. The same day she set herself apart from Sizer's Sister Michael, Sheila was talking in my presence with Ralph, her department chair, about their goals in teaching. What became clear to me, as I reviewed that session much later, was that the two of them were talking about totally different aims, although the difference between them had not yet become the problem it would become by early November. Ralph was saying that he wanted the students to know "great books"; Sheila said she wanted them to find books they liked. Ralph wanted them to be able to talk about classic characteristics of greatness, and Sheila wanted them to feel confident about reading and talking about what they liked and what they didn't like and why. Those fundamental differences were to cause severe distress for Sheila. Who was right? What should she be doing?

On August 24, 1989, she told me, "I need to give up having to comment on everything that gets said." Well before the end of our 2 years together, she had come to understand from her own experience of talking on tape the value of being heard. She determined to let that happen for all students, even the shy ones who would never dare say something to the whole class. She was pleased to see small groups providing a first forum for real conversation in which students could enjoy essentially uninterrupted sorting through of feelings and ideas. She took time to work with students on really listening to one another in those groups. Staying out of the conversation herself was not easy, especially when the small groups reassembled to report and reflect together as a whole group. After all, she had been trained to do what was called "leading" the discussions: "I'm really confused, because there are times when I *talk,* and I think I'm trying to find a way to get *them* talking. I'm struggling, but I'm trying. I was *trained* to ask leading questions" (November 15, 1989).

In September of 1989, she had commented on the unnatural situation that a classroom is: "We're taught you stand in front of the room and have everyone quiet. Well, if you're at a party or you're with people or working on something, you're not quiet. You're busy talking."

Her impulse to jump in troubled her, because she saw that her talk dominated theirs. Having read David Johnson and Roger Johnson's (1975) *Learning Together and Alone* over the summer of 1989, however, she was beginning to see her behavior as a remnant of traditional teachers' unbelief that students can "get it" without teacher intervention. In a three-way conversation over lunch on November 13, 1989, Sheila and Ralph were talking again about her talking too much. He had to admit the tendency about himself as well: "We *all* tend to preach—we get excited!" By keeping the construction of knowledge, accompanied by the talking and getting excited, for him- or herself, they admitted with some personal regret that the teacher effectively deprives the students of that experience (Adams & Horton, 1975; Belenky, Clinchy, Goldberger, & Tarule, 1986; Collins & Seidman, 1980; Culley & Portuges, 1985; Freire, 1968).

Although Ralph could see the fault in Sheila, she felt that he and others did not always see it in themselves. She told me on November 15 that most of the talk she heard coming out of classrooms was teacher-talk. What she understood, well before the end of the second year of the study, was that here again she needed to find a balance. She decided that her own inclination and that of other teachers to talk was a thing to be valued as well as to restrain. Teachers, she told me after the study was completed, "have to model saying things that are hard to say. They need to take a risk. They should not be silent. That's my role in life: I take risks, and [students] see that's OK."

The tension she felt had to do with her conviction that teachers don't let students talk enough, that their own talk dominates, and that it is not always at appropriate times. Sheila had administrative support for her perception that students need to talk ideas through with one another. The principal of VCRHS, Ernest, was also looking for the buzz of conversation that meant to him that real learning was going on. Of the school's decision in the early 1980s to move to heterogeneous grouping, Ernest told me how excited he had been to overhear faculty conversations stimulated by a course, "Models of Teaching," being taught on-site at VCRHS by one of the university professors:

> We had about 15, 16 participants in that course, and it started discussion going in the faculty room about, "I introduced this material using this model, and it worked out great. How did it work with you?"
>
> And back and forth. The dialogue was just neat—to walk into the faculty room and hear these people talking in this way. (February 12, 1990)

What he had seen among some members of his faculty was what Sheila was now seeing with her students.

Ernest told me that the original idea for change to heterogeneous grouping had been sparked by the need to evaluate the school for accreditation. The verbalizing of what needed to happen, he said, was the process that ". . . emboldened the people who were feeling that way to kind of find out if we couldn't make some changes" (February 12, 1990).

Clearly, both Ernest and Sheila understood talk to be empowerment. By March 5, 1990, Sheila trusted that if they talked enough about an issue, students would arrive at clarity and understanding of a text and of themselves. Through talking to a respectful and patient audience, she had come to believe, they would come up against their own sometimes narrow assumptions, and hear themselves change. The same with grammar. Students needed only practice with talk and with writing—that is, with trusting their own voices: "Or if a lot of times a kid is writing something that's not working I'll say, 'Well, tell me what it is,' because they'll *say* it correctly. And then I'll just say, 'Write that down' " (March 20, 1990).

Our ongoing dialoguing had helped Sheila to see her situation in a larger context. Increasingly, research studies and personal accounts reveal that most teachers start out having been conditioned by years of unconscious participation to behave in traditional ways. Teachers who choose alternative structures report relapsing into traditional behavior when they feel fatigued, preoccupied, or threatened:

> I became so nervous about entering a new realm that I unconsciously slipped into one of the most comfortable postures of . . . pedagogy: at the moment I sat down in front of the students I became an *expert in the field.* (Bezucha, 1985, p. 86)

Changing the rules about classroom relationships at the high school or college level is not easy for teachers or for students.

The Factory Model

My original research found that the traditional teaching role in large part reproduces the hierarchical authoritarian family model. The other dominant model, equally pervasive as well as equally oppressive, is the sense of the school as factory or business (Bowles & Gintis, 1976; Callahan, 1962; Grumet, 1988). Factories above all value product over both human being and process, make little or no space for caring relationships or even genuine conversation, and reward speed and efficiency over reflectiveness and the necessary messiness of creativity. In both factories and high school teaching, the idea is for the person in charge to be in full control, with everything running smoothly. In the factory situation, workers are always aware that, as they engage in tasks chosen by someone other than themselves, someone with power to judge and discipline is always watching suspiciously (Sennett & Cobb, 1972). Students report feeling as if they are on an assembly line during the whole of their schooling, particularly in high school.

As a result of many years of regularized socialization by the two forces authoritarian control and "the cult of efficiency" (Callahan, 1962), it is not surprising that most teachers doubt the appropriateness of nurturing for a secondary school environment. Sheila, however, had experienced at least one nurturing high school teacher who had taken the time to get to know and care about her students as individuals. This teacher had encouraged students to dare to question, speak out, listen to themselves and one another as well as to her, and read and think divergently. Sheila talked about this teacher throughout the 2 years of this study, indicating that she saw herself following her example.

Teaching as a relationship was something that Ernest, the principal at VCRHS, recognized in other terms. He told me in February of 1989 that he was grateful to observe the nurturing approach of special education teachers. Unlike most of those other members of the faculty he termed "academic" faculty, special educators perceived their role as focusing not on texts but on the children. From that perspective, their voices had been the most persuasive in arguing for heterogeneous grouping.

The freedom of a special education teacher to focus on children rather than on content is partly a function of what Sheila had cynically observed: No one really expects much of those children, so the pressure to produce a quality-controlled product is off. Although Sheila and Ernest saw attributes in special education classrooms that proponents of student-centered teaching would welcome for their students, "regular" high school teachers are supposed to be "tough." Relieving the classroom of pressure and being personally gentle, supportive, and attentive to students' needs is seen as being "easy," which Sheila discovered is interpreted from the outside as "lacking in rigor." Both preservice and practicing teachers often say they fear that they will lose the students' respect or lose control if they allow for the unpredictability of feelings. The nontraditional structure of a student-centered classroom looks like chaos until the viewer can find the pattern (Ashton-Warner, 1963; Rogers, 1973). The unspoken ethic of control in the high school, however benign, felt like pressure on Sheila to play a role in spite of her instincts to be herself. She resisted that pressure, but not without cost:

> I'm *going* to touch kids. I'm going to whisper in their ear. I am willing to buy them presents, because that's the way that I am. It's the way that I am as a teacher, it's the way that I am as a person, and I feel like I—I almost feel sometimes like I'm supposed to walk in the building and leave my person elsewhere, and be this other thing. (December 18, 1989)

It Is OK to Be a Mother

Sheila's regained confidence in her own choices as a teacher had been buoyed by hearing of student-centered learning research study results and, in particular, some of the intensive recent scholarship on how women learn (Belenky et al., 1986; Culley, Diamond, Edwards, Lennox, & Portuges, 1985; Gilligan, 1982; Rich, 1979). This scholarship appealed to Sheila because it called into question the role of teacher as expert and imparter of a received body of knowledge. Preferring to encourage student interaction and cooperation as ways for students to understand the meaning of their own lived experience as a valid part of any text, "feminist pedagogy," practiced by men as well as women, is student centered, requiring a transformed role for the teacher.

This alternative pedagogy acknowledges and offers a correction to a reality that had distressed Sheila deeply: the traditional passivity of students, particularly girls. In terms of content, this scholarship recognizes the richness and legitimacy of the lived stories of both teachers and students. It validates what Sheila had learned to trust. In terms of process, the new thinking openly calls for mutually respectful conversation or dialogue instead of debate (Raymond, 1985;

Rifkin, 1985; Snoek, 1985). The emergent guidelines for student-centered processes sound like best practices in elementary schools; they also sound like the way a nurturing parent is with his or her children:

- Make the material, and yourself, real and accessible while maintaining "firm enough ego boundaries" (Portuges, 1985, p. 184) to work through the problems texts offer
- Listen to the students
- Stay unobtrusively available while they learn to listen to one another
- Be careful not to reproduce structures that humiliated them in the past
- Move the furniture to allow for interaction and join them where they are
- Do not let anyone dominate or get marginalized
- Make engagement with texts personal and concrete rather than abstract
- Do not rush them—focus on process rather than on the product and give it time, even when it is not working well
- Allow them to make choices and to set their own agendas within the framework of your larger vision, which has to be *their* growth rather than your ego
- Cultivate tolerance for ambiguity
- Help them learn what they need to learn in order to operate in the world
- Help them challenge illegitimate authority without losing their grounding, by designing ways for them to look for connectedness
- Allow them to develop and appreciate their own voices
- Let their own lives, and yours, be at least part of the text that is studied

Carrying theory into practice is by no means easy. All theorists attempting it describe personal struggle against internalized traditional schooling.

Despite such influences for student-centeredness from outside Sheila's school, these were not as powerful as the pressure of colleagues and structures against it. One VCRHS teacher told her angrily, "The research is wrong!" when she attempted to defend her use of cooperative learning. Most other teachers were less dramatic in their cynicism, but the tone of disapproval that seemed to surround her directly felt overwhelming.

Nevertheless, over time, voices from outside her day-to-day adult interactions at VCRHS supported the undeniable evidence of increasingly successful learning and community within her classroom. These voices reinforced her conscious decision to avoid her detractors and concentrate on working well with her students. On December 17, 1989, she decided, "Maybe I just have to accept that I'm a mother—that's who I am—even if the men hate it."

Patience:
Seeing Teaching as a Process,
Not a Performance or a Product

Sheila was willing to work against her own habits of teacher-centeredness, and then of content-centeredness, because she already felt comfortable with the attitudes that seem to be preconditions for student-centered teaching. She already trusted in both students and interactive processes, despite the doubts that the dominant culture of the school had about both. Describing herself as normally impatient and dissatisfied with less than total participation, Sheila nevertheless found herself willing to try to be patient with both the students and herself as the new skills were learned and practiced. Determined to focus on the positive aspects of all their interactions, Sheila used her students' initial resistance to new ways of working as information about how to help everyone in her classes—including herself—move forward.

Early in our collaboration, during a break between two classes that were reading abstract and difficult U.S. Revolutionary War speeches (January 17, 1989), Sheila and I discussed her students' uncertainty about how to proceed. I suggested she might break down the tasks into more manageable sizes. Accordingly, she revised her instructions to the students in her very next class. She tried out jigsawing parts of the assignment (Aronson, 1978), giving each group a section to focus on and share about, rather than asking everyone to look at everything. She encouraged them to use one another as resources, raising their hands for her help only for things that the group had determined it could not figure out. After they had formed into groups, she went around helping those groups rearrange their desks for more connection within and more distance between the separate groups. When two groups of two wanted to work together as four even though they had different things to do, she acknowledged that they could collaborate "for the first question." She said to them, "You need those people? OK!"

All of these were subtleties she was trying out for the first time. It was not a perfect class. Predictably, in part because the material was so abstract, traditional habits persisted: individualism, search for right answers, and dependence on the teacher. Three girls were facing each other but reading and writing separately. In a mixed group of three, the two boys were doing most of the work. In another mixed group, a girl told Sheila, "I need some help. I don't know what I'm looking for." She had not thought to consult with people in her group. When Sheila tried to get the other two to help, they were frustrated as well. Throughout the class, there was not much real conversation or discussion. People seemed to be searching their texts for right answers, sometimes not even trusting one another to help them find those. In the group closest to where I was sitting, people were asking one another, "What did you put?" Some were ready to give up.

By my next visit (February 14, 1989), Sheila was struggling with herself to stay back as students resisted the unfamiliar process of constructing their own meaning. In an early class, students were choosing modular courses for the fall semester. Many were uncomfortable with choosing. One girl asked Sheila, "Why do you give us all this responsibility? Why don't you just stick us in a class?" In response to their expressions of dissatisfaction with the choices, Sheila suggested, "If you're complaining, design a course in your notebook."

In the class that followed, setting up presentations on Cooper, Irving, and Bryant, the groups were still not working perfectly; in fact, there was considerable wasting of time, but Sheila obviously had determined to be patient. This class was the first in which I noticed her watching from a careful distance, recording how they were operating, letting them work, and trying not to interfere. When they came back to the large group, she gave back to them what she had seen: that they hadn't gotten far—"How do you think the groups were operating? How could we do it better?" Some students were defensive, ready with the traditional punishment for themselves: "Give a quiz." Sheila suggested having a scribe in each group, reminding them that 50% of their grade was for cooperation. She was determined that they would take responsibility for their own presentations and determined to discipline herself to let them do that.

In the next class I observed (March 7, 1989), Sheila showed me that she had accepted the long-term nature of helping the students through their resistance to a student-centered process. She briefly joined a group that was asking, "So, what are we supposed to do?" Acknowledging that they were confused, she invited, "Ask me a question," to get them to be specific about what they thought they needed before they could move forward. Their questions revealed that they were stuck, not on aspects of substance in *The Adventures of Huckleberry Finn* (Twain, 1884/1981) but on issues of form: "How long should it be?" and "Do we have to do three examples?" At the end of almost 20 minutes of her going around trying to get them to tell one another what they thought, Sheila asked them all to return to their own chairs in the original rows and told them, "I'm not so sure that that time was well spent, but this is what I learned." Essentially, what she had learned was that the task needed smaller groups and more thought about who works with whom.

More important than those specifics was that instead of blaming them, she was sharing with them her thinking about how to make the process work better. What she told me afterward revealed her confidence: "Next time they'll do better," and "I need to model alternative ways of presenting information." She did not panic about their not having learned what they were "supposed to" in the precious class time. She did not consider it a waste, because she had done some important learning: "I'm letting them fumble a lot. . . . I try to keep reminding myself that when you do things kids aren't used to, you have to be patient."

That she did it is not to say that it was easy for her. During that March 7 visit, she told me of one of her own reservations: "The bad part is I want to know what they're talking about." On the phone the next week, she hoped, "Maybe next week everything will click in. It's based on fear, primarily—that they can't do it." On March 31, she told me how hard it was:

> I think what you have to realize about grouping, as far as I'm concerned, is that there are great moments, and then they'll take two steps back and they'll be horrible again.

> I think, I know for me, I just have to remind myself of
> those things so I'm not totally discouraged that they're not
> doing anything. They *are* doing something.

She continued to try in spite of how hard it was, because she basically
trusted the process: students' writing would help them discover
what they thought, as would having to explain and to listen to others.
On May 9, 1989, she said, "I've watched kids change their minds on
issues when they're presented with other choices."

Using our conversations as a place to reflect, Sheila looked at
both the negatives and the positives of a class session, figuring out
for herself what would make it go better next time. There were a lot
of "Maybe I should" kinds of statements about what options might
work. On May 15, 1989, her assessment of the year that would soon
be ending was positive and forward looking:

> You know, I'm still frustrated. Some of them, I think, I could
> have done better. It took me a little while to get in gear, and
> even now I look at a lesson and I think, I could probably do
> this differently, but I would say, overall, if I were to be really
> fair to them, they've done a really good job. They've come a
> long way, and I'm going to tell them.

And at the very end of the year, she said, "I think next year will be
better. I think it's going to be a lot better. I hope" (June 16, 1989).
Already by May and certainly during June and the summer, Sheila
was talking about next steps for both herself and her classes.

On September 18, 1989, her comments revealed pleasure that her
patience and restraint had been worth the effort. She said of her students, "They're struggling, but I'm really impressed with them"; "I'll
be interested to see how they work together"; and "I think that they're
doing OK." Of herself she said, "I feel like this is the year I'll get
better at organizing the processes. I'm practicing giving them time"
(September 10, 1989).

She could be patient with herself, as well as with her students,
for how long it was taking to unlearn traditional habits and learn
new ones. Over the summer, she had read materials on cooperative
learning:

It's OK that I don't know how to do cooperative learning—I wasn't taught. I didn't learn how to be a teacher. I'm learning now. My instinct with relating to people is for them to talk to each other, but we're taught you have to be in control and they have to be quiet. (September 10, 1989)

She was now working to overcome her instinct to protect her students from confusion:

I'm learning to deal with silence. I wanted to jump in. I want to be patient with them not knowing. It's hard to have them struggle—it's my job to help them! I have to get over feeling that, and just let them struggle. (September 18, 1989)

Sheila's working through of her own and her students' reservations might have characterized the struggle for change throughout the English department, as Ralph perceived their efforts. He said that the other teachers "are learning that the process has to be trained." They were learning, he said, that students "can get there if they're given the time to get there." But there were cautions, even in that mid-September conversation in 1989, which prefigured later conflicts between Sheila and the rest of the department. Sheila said, "The kids perceive us as easy because there's no pressure." Furthermore, Ralph said two things that were to get in his way that year. Of the students he said, "They're not sure what questions they want to ask"; of himself, he said, "If I set it up correctly, they don't need me, and I'm lonely."

By the fall semester, Sheila had almost dealt with being left out of the students' small-group conversations. She did not yet completely trust that between her active but respectful eavesdropping and their later reporting of findings she would know what was being said beyond what was in the reader-response notebooks. Perhaps more important was the loneliness Ralph mentioned: She missed the full-time contact with her students.

Her successful preparation of the students, however, was apparent. On November 13, 1989, the small groups in the first class I observed got to work immediately on tasks about which they were very clear. Each group had one character from *Lord of the Flies* (Golding, 1954). Arguing within the groups was animated but personally respectful. Once they had made decisions, a spokesperson for each group went up to write the decisions on the board. Everyone else began to take down the information their peers had collected. When it was all up there, Sheila asked the spokespeople to talk about what they had put on the board and then asked everyone to focus on the larger task. According to the information they had so far, they were to predict whether a particular character would survive or not. They spent the entire period making this one decision. The energy level and the sense of accomplishment felt powerful.

At the end of that day's classes, Sheila knew what she wanted to work on next: (a) to figure out better ways to balance between spontaneity and having students listen to one another and (b) to let go of her own need for personal contact with them. She had worked through both of those by the end of June 1990 and again was ready to take what she defined as the next steps for her own development as a teacher.

What It Means to Be Student Centered: Looking At How Kids Learn Rather Than What There Is to Teach

The strongest force compelling Sheila to take the risks involved in conducting a student-centered classroom was her own direct experience with her students' capacity for complex, intense, and rigorous thinking once they had developed the confidence and the procedures for exploring texts. She trusted the insights their explorations gave both her and them about their lives.

In a May 9, 1989, class on "The Lady or the Tiger" (Stockton, 1893), the small-group task was to decide what the lady chose and to back up their choices. When students came back into the large session, they were to hear from one another. Then they would decide whether and why they liked each choice and whether the choice made sense, given the story.

What the students came up with suggested that they had indeed engaged in the story. Many of them spoke from an understanding of the force of jealousy in their own lives. One group was cynical about how the man trusted the princess's love for him. One student said, "I'd do the same thing!" Another talked about a selfish woman. Dave decided to rewrite: If it was a story about a woman choosing a man or a tiger, he would let her get the man and then shoot him. No one took the leap of breaking through the initial dualism and suggesting a third option of any kind, and no one talked about woman hating, so Sheila did not raise those possibilities: She allowed all that they said, and they walked out of the class talking about what they would do in the same situation.

Sheila felt that was why she was teaching literature. She wanted young people to look at the choices people make in their lives and at the consequences of those choices. She wanted them to test out, in the safety of their minds and imaginations, all the possible ways they might behave in similar situations.

Almost every class period, students came up with ideas that Sheila had not considered on her own, and she told them so. Not wanting to be seen as an expert on the literature was not a matter of not trusting her own sophistication as a reader. Indeed, she considered herself a widely read and very competent reader. But she cared about students' engagement with the works rather than about the works themselves. What could they learn from literature that would help them live their lives? And what could she learn from them? She was honestly interested in what they thought.

Not every piece of literature, to be sure, offered such openendedness as "The Lady or the Tiger" (Stockton, 1893). Because there were no right answers, it was a good choice for students' practice of having their own direct, personal experience with a story. Again stressing that there were no right answers, she made it clear that the focus she wanted them to maintain in their peer editing sessions was not on "criticizing"—which the students took to mean finding all the errors—but on what they got out of one another's papers and how to make them and their own clearer and stronger.

To make the total system work, she changed her method of evaluation almost immediately after our working together began to give her a theoretical grounding for her instincts. She stopped testing on literature in February of 1989, deciding to read only the readerresponse notebooks. She let the groups choose what to focus on, and she gave 50% of their grade for cooperation. She wanted them to struggle with what was confusing in the books, and she urged them toward, and gave them credit for, using one another as resources. Some late 1989 and early 1990 exams, she had decided, would be to engage with some new text and talk to one another about it. In other classes, she decided to use anthologies of their own writing as texts on which to base exams.

Protecting Without Taking Over

In all the class sessions I observed over the 2-year study, even before she began to practice specific cooperative-learning strategies, Sheila's physical presence in her own classroom was with the students rather than distanced from them as if she embodied her own commitment to be discovering along with them (Freire, 1968). When the seating was in rows, she would be moving around the room as they talked, often sitting on top of uninhabited desks not just at the margins but right within the rows. She tried to be at the front only when she was writing instructions or recording their findings on the board. Her moving around made it necessary for whoever was talking to turn around toward her, so a student's comments were usually audible to everyone, even a visitor at the back of the room.

In spite of her efforts at inclusiveness, however, my early observations confirmed her experience of boys' domination of classroom conversations. Small-group decision-making work turned out to be the solution she had sought: to create space for the girls to contribute as well and do their learning by talking through their ideas.

As early as February 14, 1989, Sheila was urging students to be resources for one another: "If you're struggling, the best place to go is to the people in your group." She respected their choices, sometimes letting go of a certain theme or issue from a book if no group chose it and sometimes offering to explore it herself as her own contribution to the conversation. Protecting them from the frustration of not knowing what to do but allowing them to struggle with their texts, Sheila's instructions for group work indicated that she had tried to anticipate every eventuality when she was designing her lessons. According to the students I interviewed in both December of 1989 and March of 1990:

> She tells you exactly what she wants you to do, so when you get in your groups everybody understands. (December 18, 1989)

> I don't know, the way she explains herself you really understand what you're doing. (March 5, 1990)

She effectively balanced trusting students' responsibility for their own learning with her own accessibility: She did not abandon them as they worked. As early as March 1989, she moved around among the groups to check on how they were doing, encouraging: "You're doing a really nice job of talking to each other." She would check in more frequently with students who tended to get distracted without her monitoring.

Sheila's students were grateful that her reading of their daily response journals and her alert attention to tone and dynamic as they worked in their groups allowed her to know exactly who was doing what in every group. Therefore, they felt protected from exploitation, reporting that in her class, unlike some others that used small-group work, "hitchhikers" could not depend on one person to do all the work. That was something she worked at. I noticed Dave leaning back, away from the intense conversation between his group members, Paula and Jen. In reply to my question about that, Sheila mused,

> I don't know. He said he was giving them information. What I'm going to do tomorrow is he's going to have to write everything down. See, I'm making him work with them, and he doesn't want to, 'cause he can't just fool around, basically.
>
> But next time to really fully engage him he's going to be the notetaker. 'Cause Dave has trouble. He struggles a lot. He wants to just fool around and have fun. He has to stay after Tuesday, 'cause he's not doing the work to my satisfaction, and it's really hard. He wants it to be easy.
>
> But actually I really like him, so we'll figure it out. (March 20, 1990)

The Role of a Teacher

On June 16, 1989, Sheila talked to me at length about how far she had come in her thinking about the role of a teacher. The student-centered strategies now came naturally to her, she maintained again on November 10, 1989: "I remembered that I *do* like it. That's the funny part, that I like my students. So when I remember that about them, it's fun. There's not as much pressure."

When she did things her own way, rather than the way she saw other teachers around her teaching, she enjoyed her work: "When we relax together, the work gets done, everyone has fun, it's not a big deal." Still, she was intensely aware that her view of her role was different from that of teachers she saw:

I think teachers feel that . . . their job is to be in charge. I guess I just don't feel that way. I really think that in a class, we're sort of in it together. I don't feel superior. I don't feel better. I just feel like I would like to be a facilitator of kids finding things that they're interested in doing.

That's why it seems to me that it makes a lot of sense to have kids choosing their own reading, and kids talking to each other about the books that they read . . . just sort of sharing about things on their own level where they are.

Because I feel that where I am in my life, I'm not necessarily interested in what they're interested in, in terms of their reading. But it needs to be where they are.

Always, she was aware of the reality of her students' 14- to 18-year-old lives. She had given up thinking in terms of tracking before she got to VCRHS. As a result, she treated all the students as competent. She knew their individual strengths and insecurities. Sheila felt that they lived up to her expectations. From their own testimony, the students felt her respect for them. By April 27, 1990, Sheila was confident that she could set an agenda and design activities so that the best would come out of her students. She defined a good class:

It's good because everyone is working together in a positive way. We're helping each other out. . . . I really didn't do anything except allow for that to happen. I'll bring out the best in people because that's what I'm looking for.

As later chapters will describe, there were times, especially at the beginning of the study, when Sheila's focus tended to be on what did not go well in a class rather than on what did. In those cases, she used my feedback to redirect her focus toward the essentially positive context of disappointing moments. By the end of the school year 1989-1990, she was seeing things that did not work well as things she would not worry about, but would take responsibility for making better:

I know one of the things that I really need to work on is boys—9th-, 10th-grade boys—and what they need in the classroom and how to channel a lot of the energy that I often find negative or silly or stupid. They grate on me. They rub me the wrong way and then I get angry and then they get angry. It's like a real cyclical thing.

And that's something that I need to be thinking about. But I notice that when they're working on something that they're really into or they really like, there are no difficulties. (May 24, 1990)

In every instance when things did not go well in a class or when she perceived the students to be "out of control," her instinct was to adjust herself, not them:

I can clearly see . . . what a struggle they have trying to en-gage in material they're not ready for. But there's other stuff they *are* ready for, and their own writing really engages them. They want to be telling their own stories, which is OK.

So when I get off of—I fight with them when I try to control the group when I want them to listen to me. They can*not* listen to me for more than 5 minutes, some of those boys. So I have to limit, and if I limit it they will. They're pretty attentive. But it took me a while to figure that out. (May 24, 1990)

As she described her own classroom, Sheila recognized how far she had come toward realizing her own vision: "I think I have often been in kids' way to get things done, and this year I've noticed that I've been very willing to get out of the way and have been happy with what has happened" (May 24, 1990).

She could even let go of her unrealistic expectations for her colleagues when she realized that most teachers, as students them-selves in predominantly traditional classrooms, would not have directly experienced there the mutual respect, responsibility, con-fidence, and sense of community that a student-centered classroom works at developing. She came to understand through her experience of our collaboration that time and support are needed if teachers are to envision new roles along with new structures for themselves and their classrooms.

The most helpful perspective we generated together was think-ing of the importance of her student-centered work for the next generation of teachers. They would not be conditioned to one-right-answer thinking, such that if someone else was right, they would have to be wrong. They would not fear one another's judgment or help. They would not need to know everything or pretend to know everything to keep the respect of their students or colleagues. They would not have to operate within safely prescribed boundaries.

Sheila's vision of what she hoped students would take from her classes did not change fundamentally over the 2 years during which I observed and listened to her. What changed over time was the range of strategies she was able to develop to achieve her goals, and her confidence that her agenda was a worthy one.

5 Colliding With "Institutional Realities"

The Struggle to Swim Upstream

My decision was to focus on Sheila's work, her developing perception of it, and the multiple perceptions of it among some of her students and some of her colleagues. This decision necessitated a further methodological choice not to take a broader in-depth look at the other faculty members at VCRHS who had also made a serious commitment to try to work in more student-centered ways. Visiting only two classes each of two other teachers and interviewing those two only twice each, I could not glean as much information about them as I was getting about Sheila from multiple visits and interviews.

I will not presume, therefore, to draw conclusions about their teaching or their understanding of the nature of teaching from the limited amount of data I accumulated from what they said to me and what I actually saw. What is important for this study is Sheila's view of the extent to which her vision was shared within the school and thus the extent to which she felt personally and professionally supported at VCRHS. Most of what I saw and will report was through the prism of Sheila's feelings.

In both of his long interviews with me, Ralph mentioned that he and his English department were "all in this together" and that they were "all just learning how to do this." However, Sheila's perception was that because he never shared with her his own feelings of uncertainty, he did not feel at all unsure of himself as he went about "just learning how to do this." Whenever he spoke with her, as she reported it, he spoke only of how difficult it was to train the students to this new kind of working, not of his own version of what she was experiencing, not of his internal struggle against habits conditioned by years of successful teaching in the traditional mode. As this chapter will show, because Ralph and other teachers did not mention or seem to be dealing with internal struggles, Sheila felt almost totally isolated in hers.

Certain social forces contributed to the alienation that affected Sheila so strongly. As the literature since Lortie (1975) indicates, one of the most distressing realities of a school, particularly a secondary school, is the physical constraint of time and space that keeps teachers from interacting naturally with one another.

The literature on cooperative learning (see Resources on Student-Centered Teaching at the end of this book) indicates further that habits of individualism and competitiveness are deeply bred into students. These habits reinforce the structural distance among professionals, who in many cases were successful as students within individualistic and competitive classroom systems. In traditional classrooms, students do not generally develop the kind of trust in one another that would allow them to admit to not knowing something or to not being quite sure of what they are doing. Adults who have become teachers still carry those habits with them, and may operate from them under the pressure of a role that seems to require them to be experts. In traditional classrooms, from which most teachers come, to ask for or give help is considered "cheating." Habits of supporting or asking for support are not developed.

Thus, teachers tend to be wary of one another. Most expect that they will be judged by the next teacher on the basis of their present students' academic preparation. None of those forces contribute to the kind of open sharing of delight in the students nor, to be sure, the sharing of uncertainty and sense of struggle, which would have made Sheila feel "normal" at the school.

Expectations

Almost as soon as she began teaching at VCRHS in the fall of 1988, Sheila's sense of herself as a teacher was being daily shaken by the collision between what she had expected and what she was actually experiencing in the school. Basically, her discouragement with herself, her students, and her colleagues had to do with what turned out to be a set of unrealistic expectations. She felt that she had been assured she would be joining a faculty fully committed to heterogeneous grouping and fully engaged in innovative teaching methods to make that kind of grouping work best for all students. What she perceived instead was that most of the teachers in the school were still teaching in ways that seemed quite traditional to her. She was confused. Maybe what they were doing was what the school wanted and she was wrong?

As she watched and listened to other teachers, it seemed to her that no one else was uncertain; no one else talked about making mistakes. She, on the other hand, had daily uncertainties and doubts as she worked to overcome the resistance of her traditionally trained students to the new processes she was introducing. There seemed to be no one to talk with about the kinds of situations she was experiencing in her classroom. Everyone else seemed satisfied. Everyone else's classes were great.

She became afraid to expose her sense of inadequacy for fear the other teachers would condemn her. In fact, she felt criticism on many sides, but an absence of balancing encouragement, even from the principal whose ideals agreed with hers in the abstract. He was too busy to give her the concrete feedback and affirmation that she felt she needed. Increasingly, she felt like an outcast: "I don't fit in here."

Marginalization was not the position she had been led to expect to have to occupy. She had not prepared herself to retain her centeredness when she sensed disapproval, particularly that of her department chair Ralph, because as she understood but could not yet overcome, she had been trained to seek the approval of authority. When a series of systematic taped interviews began to replace our earlier, less formal dialogues on March 31, 1990, she already was working on this issue. There would be some things about her that people would not like.

At her previous school at which the students she taught had been labeled "lower ability," people did not seem to check on whether she was preparing students formally to meet a series of next teachers' expectations. She had felt free to allow the learning to take place naturally. Here, on the other hand, the specter of a different kind of accountability for what students would be measured on felt threatening to her. In her recurrent vulnerable times, she wondered if she was a "bad teacher." She could say she was being "paranoid," but the uncertainty itself frightened her: "I don't know, I can't tell"; "What if . . .?"; and "It's scary when you try new things."

Her extreme self-doubt carried over to our research project together. The September 1989 interview was one of several in which she expressed fear that I had picked the wrong person to watch and that her mistakes would "mess up" my study. I had to reassure her more than once that my interest was in documenting the struggle and seeing the process, rather than observing a "perfect" teacher.

Once she began to look back on that paranoia in January 1990, she described her thinking about the whole first year and a half:

> So I get into a school and I think, what am I supposed to do? So I look around at what the other people are doing, and part of me just thinks I need to do it that way because maybe I think I'm supposed to do it that way. . . . I could do that, but so what? I don't get it.
>
> But then I think, maybe, no: *I* know about hyperbole. Maybe [the students] should know it. Does that make someone smart? I don't know. Does that make them culturally literate? In whose culture?
>
> Who's deciding what things are important? That's another thing that's just a kicker. I don't know.

Adjusting the Focus

Dissatisfaction with herself was deeper than others could feel about her; Sheila's expectations of herself with her students were extremely high. As successful as even the very first class sessions I saw her teach seemed to my eye, she came out of them expressing disappointment:

> I feel frustrated. I try things and they don't work. I want intense discussion. I start to think that I'm not a good teacher. I feel like I have to do what other people do to survive the day, and I hate myself. Maybe I'm *not* good. They're bored, they hate the reading, they're lazy, they want to watch TV.

It's easier to just give information out. I can do that.
That's what I mean by compromising. I don't know the steps.
They don't want to think. They demand grades. Some kids
can't read *Scarlet Letter* (Hawthorne, 1850/1981). Talking to
each other is how they get it, but they won't *do* that.

Liz   What are your expectations?
Sheila I don't know—I want to reach *everybody*. I don't want to
lose *any*body. (October 16, 1988)

The November 22 class on *The Scarlet Letter* (Hawthorne, 1850/
1981) (described on p. 19) did not meet her expectation of "total interaction." Coming out of the December 6 class on *The Crucible*
(Miller, 1953) (described on pp. 19-20), she apologized to me for some
students' saturation with too many papers to listen to: "I want them
to be perfect!"

This expectation of perfection represented what Sheila came to
recognize as her tendency to focus on the almost insignificant flaws
in an otherwise overwhelmingly positive experience. In the process
of overcoming internal pressures that blocked her vision, the first
step was for her to become aware that the disappointment she felt
was a function of her own unrealistic expectations of herself and her
students.

Our work together gave her solid strategies for avoiding the kind
of situation in which students had to listen and respond attentively
for such a sustained time as they had been asked to do during *The
Crucible* (Miller, 1953) discussion. It also allowed her to reflect on,
name, and let go of the traditional sources of her own perfectionism,
which underlay her assumption that if a class wasn't totally good, it
was totally bad. This was one of the first habits that she overcame as
she realized that demanding perfection for herself and her students
interfered with the achievement of her vision of learning as process
rather than product.

The outcome of her having made a conscious decision to focus
on what went well in a class session was surprising to her, but would
not be so surprising to observers familiar with the literature on and
practice of student-centered teaching. By the end of the study, Sheila
noticed that without her expecting or even thinking much about it
anymore, she was achieving almost 100% participation in all of her
classes.

The Expectation of
Heterogeneous Grouping

Sheila's expectation that her values would be widely shared and already in practice in the school was based on VCRHS's recent history of restructuring. According to Ernest, the principal (February 12, 1990), a decision had been made in 1981-1982 that the school would not use any system of tracking (February 12, 1990). The impetus had come from the guidance counselors; the librarians; and teachers of remedial reading, art, industrial arts, home economics, and the resource room. These were people who saw students one-on-one or "as a mix" and observed that lower-tracked students characteristically had low self-esteem. What that meant for these teachers was that the school was not doing the job it ought to do. They began to talk to one another and to Ernest, who knew the research on tracking versus heterogeneous grouping and had been hoping for this kind of change in his school. He also knew that the change could not come from the top; the teachers themselves had to support it fully.

Some of the regular classroom teachers, particularly in math and science, resisted the notion that it was possible to "get across a body of knowledge" in a classroom in which abilities were widely mixed. But enough teachers wanted to do it, so it was recommended that the school try heterogeneous grouping, starting at the junior high school level. The school committee, as Ernest described it, was not difficult to persuade for an important reason: "There were some people who were very supportive of it—school committee people who either had kids who were in the low tracks or remembered when they were in the low tracks themselves" (February 12, 1990).

He had noticed an interesting fact about the adult population of the feeder towns to VCRHS:

> The people that are college bound in your top track, they move away to all over the country to college, and they seldom return to their home town. The people who stay in the community, and eventually become the school committee people themselves, were in the low tracks. (February 12, 1990)

The factor that reinforced the school committee's inclination to try heterogeneous grouping was the number of the teachers who were fully committed to the idea. What happened then was surprising:

By the time we got into it, the English department, which was the critical department to make the changes, they were ready to try it through the whole 7-12. And so we kind of jumped into it faster than we probably should have, in hindsight, but it worked out. (February 12, 1990)

Thus, the conviction that she was moving into a department already in the vanguard of a school in a dynamic process of change might have been a reasonable one when Sheila started teaching at VCRHS in September 1988. Perhaps she took Ernest's own total commitment to heterogeneous grouping as representative of the entire faculty. What Ernest already knew about pockets of resistance within the faculty was something Sheila was to discover for herself, with the accompanying disillusionment that this study describes.

Ernest and Sheila were in agreement about the connection between tracking in a school and the inequities of the larger society. That is why they both felt so strongly about wanting to make the change within their school. They wanted the students and teachers to experience, in at least one small place, the equality of opportunity that America claims. It was consistent for Sheila, therefore, to be linking heterogeneous grouping and cooperative learning with the reading, writing, talking, and listening about the content she was asking her students to consider, inviting them to ask some very hard questions: "We're institutionally saying that some people are going to get more than others. We're encouraged to feel, 'as long as I'm the one getting everything, then I'm satisfied.' But is that OK? Is that OK?" (January 6, 1990).

The playing out of the social forces she described may have been represented by the example of Darrell, whose powerfully thoughtful insights I had witnessed in her classes for the entire year. Without heterogeneous grouping she said, "because of his socioeconomic background and his behavior" he would have been tracked into a lower-ability class, and probably lost.

Trying Cooperative Learning

Commitment in theory to heterogeneous grouping turned out to be an easier step for most classroom teachers than the next one: reconceptualizing the process of teaching within untracked classes. Until Sheila joined the faculty in 1988, the lecture-discussion format continued to be the unquestioned norm for most academic classes. Most teachers assumed that the new kind of grouping meant that they had to either "water down" their material and slow their pace or focus on meeting the needs of the students formerly tracked high ability. In either case, most had resigned themselves to reaching only a portion of their students.

When I started visiting VCRHS as a university supervisor of student teachers in September 1986, my efforts to encourage student teachers to become less teacher-centered were met with scorn by some of their cooperating teachers. "The university is fantasyland," a few veteran teachers in the faculty lounge told me, reminding the preservice teachers and me, "this is the real world." "Those methods don't work in high schools" was the more subtle but pervasive message of less outspoken cooperating teachers. Thus, I was surprised and delighted when the English department, spurred by one of its members who had been a student teacher there under my supervision, invited me to give a workshop on cooperative learning (April 12, 1989).

By then I had supervised many more student teachers placed there. As a result of their work, more VCRHS teachers had seen cooperative group strategies in action. I had also begun to work intensively with Sheila. Most important, the institutional commitment was there. Ralph told me that cooperative learning, for the English department, was an area in which

the front office expects us to be working. They expect when they walk into the class to see group work. They don't expect to see any lecturing going on or anything of that sort, and if they do we have to have a reason as to why we're doing it. (January 26, 1990)

When I conducted the workshop in April, I found many members of the department open to thinking in new ways about what students could do when teachers back off and give them more responsibility for their own learning. Some of them had already begun, tentatively, to experiment with groups in their classrooms. In that April session, the other English teachers brought up concerns and questions that had troubled Sheila as well but that she was actively working through. Hearing them express those doubts made her feel, finally, much less isolated.

Cooperative Learning Is Not Easy

On March 31, 1989, Sheila had asked me,

How do you avoid copying, or simply one person dominating? How do you get the kids to really talk to each other?
Because I find that's very difficult.
    I think the hardest thing for me is setting something up
so that they get the most discussion time and thinking out of
that.

Sheila was making a distinction between cooperative learning, with
its emphasis on interdependent decision making, and the kinds of
group work in which students sitting together do essentially individual work. By the end of April 1989, Sheila had already begun to have
fun with the new way of working, especially once she had let go of
the kind of "answer-pulling" (Holt, 1967) that had characterized her
content-centered approach as recently as the month before. She was
trying specific strategies that we had brainstormed together. What
she told me excitedly on the phone was, "Today, they were responsible for their own thinking! They were to take notes on each other's
statements. They were writing in their notebooks. I didn't look up—I
kept a list of who talked" (April, 1989).

It didn't always go this well. Sheila and I would be speaking
together about every 2 weeks, figuring out in very detailed ways
what activities would make sense for certain situations, with certain
groups, with certain students, and for certain books. As Chapter 6
will describe, my role was primarily that of a listener as Sheila talked
through what she wanted to do or what she would now do differently, with occasional questions or comments from what I had observed in the classroom that day. The focus of most of those later
spring 1989 interviews was on the intricate choreography of group
processes as she learned from watching and listening to students
what worked well and what seemed not to work so well.

What students themselves told me in a series of small-group interviews (April-May 1989, December 1989, and March 1990) affirmed
much of the work Sheila was trying to do. After so many years of
operating only individually or competitively, however, they were

predictably not at all convinced that the work in groups was what they wanted to be doing. Some absolutely preferred to work alone. Students carried their old fears into this new process:

> **First Student** Because if there's people that you don't know as well, I think sometimes it's like intimidating, because you're afraid of what they're going to think of your idea, or whatever.
>
> **Second Student** Like they'll probably say, "Oh, that's stupid."
>
> **First Student** Right. So it's harder, that's harder to discuss with them. (December, 1989)

But others reported liking the new arrangement:

> **Third Student** I think it's pretty good, 'cause you learn a lot from people.
>
> **Fourth Student** Not so much just the teacher; your friends, too. (December, 1989)

Mostly their objection, especially those of the formerly "top" students, was that the "less motivated" students ("somebody that can't do the work as good") were essentially hitchhiking off of *their* work. Mostly for that reason, they unanimously resented the group grades, which, according to the students I interviewed in March of 1989, Sheila did not give. They were pleased that "she likes to recognize individual abilities":

> **Student** I found myself doing everything, like rewriting the whole script and typing it all out, and everything like that, and she recognized that I did it by myself, and so the others didn't necessarily fail but they got graded for what they did and I got graded for what I did.
>
> **Liz** You thought that was fair.
>
> **Student** Yeah, I thought that was fair.

Students in those later sessions indicated that Sheila seemed always to be aware of who in any group was prepared and who was not. This was the impression I recorded every time I observed in

Sheila's classes. While students worked in their groups, she was quietly but actively eavesdropping and checking in. In our conferences after class, I would ask her about things I had noticed as groups worked. Invariably, she too had already noticed everything I mentioned. She had also thought through and made decisions about each of those things.

In our interviews, the students were telling me that in classrooms in which a teacher did not eavesdrop as intensely as Sheila did or did not require individual freewriting, the "deadbeats" got away with not doing their share of the work. The question of individual accountability plagued all the English teachers who were trying forms of cooperative learning. It was an issue that might have been addressed, perhaps in another workshop. But the funds for that did not materialize and not seeing great interest, I was hesitant to volunteer my time.

By this time, Sheila had been reading about cooperative learning[1] and knew that heterogeneous groups are one of the advantages of that process in that they offer an effective mix of gifts, learning styles, points of view, and abilities. Sheila recognized and enjoyed that diversity within her classrooms. Predictably, she found that her 9th graders who had come up through the junior high in heterogeneous groups were more willing to work with "just anyone" in a group than were some of the 12th graders who had not had significant heterogeneous experience. By all of their reports, however, they had been learning from their work, individually and together, what I knew Sheila had hoped they would learn.

Heterogeneous grouping and cooperative learning were happening in some teachers' classes and not others and in some departments and not others. This created problems for the classes in which Sheila and, tentatively, some other teachers were trying to use small-group methods. Heterogeneous grouping was incomplete because foreign language classes and advanced science and math classes effectively caused English and social studies to be retracked through scheduling. Even if that had not been the case, almost unconscious language and thought processes assuming superiority and inferiority were difficult to undo. According to Jessie, the 1990 senior class valedictorian whom I interviewed in late April of that year, a system that values verbal ability over other abilities is a kind of elitism that distresses even those who are successful in that system:

I mean this sounds really weird but you judge people. There's the smart people and the not-so-smart people, and you basically judge them by how well they read or how well they write, and there's nothing about science.

Like this friend I was talking about, he gets Ds in English all the time, but he's so smart in science and everything, but you don't even think about that, 'cause English and writing and reading is really what our whole school system is based on, and that's not fair.

I feel guilty when I get better grades, because that's only one type of learning. . . . I don't think it's fair that I get the grades that I do when some people study for a lot and they try so hard and they don't get anything.

But Where Is Everybody?

"The people I work with are very traditional thinkers" (January 14, 1990).

It took Sheila almost the whole of 2 academic years to sort out what she could reasonably expect of her colleagues at VCRHS. Whether there had been actual misrepresentation of the number and identity of teachers committed to innovative teaching, or whether Sheila misunderstood Ernest's investment to be representative of everyone's, she clearly had expected her colleagues to be working as hard as she was to find ways to implement student-centered teaching. Of her department chair Ralph, in particular, she had expected supportive feedback that would help her move forward toward realizing the vision she assumed they shared. She had assumed that the students would have been used to the kinds of innovative methods she was bringing in. But in our earliest dialogue (October 18, 1988), Sheila was in despair about the students' resistance, the failure of her own expectations, and her disappointment about having no real allies in this work: "It's hard to put the university ideas—and my own—into practice when no one else is doing it!"

Her alienation from her peers was not just in terms of what was going on in her classroom or theirs. It was not just a matter of professional differences. Personalities and styles were subject to subtle messages, to which Sheila felt vulnerable because of her other insecurities. Casual remarks about teachers who work hard and those who do not as well as other judgments of appearances, judgments based on traditional assumptions, had by the spring of 1989 begun to affect Sheila, who was working many 20-hour days:

> Well, I was walking up and down the hall a lot today because I have kids in here [study hall], . . . so [this other teacher] was teasing me, but I really wanted to say, "Come to my house some night when I'm racking my brains over how to do it and how to do it better."

Comments made to her directly in the faculty lounge frequently felt personal, even sexist, and were very disturbing to Sheila. She knew how to handle inappropriate behavior in a classroom, but not how to react when adults behaved disrespectfully to one another, especially when she herself was the target.

The cause of some of the overt hostility that she sensed toward her may have come from a source that meant well. In a phone call to me just before the new school year was to begin in 1989, Sheila said, "Ralph told the other teachers how much they're going to learn from me."

Not until we looked at that again at the end of the study did Sheila and I realize the extent to which his praise of her to other teachers might have turned out to have been a set up for her, although Ralph had not meant it to be. It was hard to see it that way then, because as Ralph told me when I interviewed him that September 1989, he and his staff felt really ready to try teaching in the new way. Both the students and the teachers, he said, would be struggling to undo the habits of traditional learning and teaching. However, the centrality of the body of knowledge did not yet seem open for negotiation for any of the teachers but Sheila, who had evolved to letting it go only with great difficulty the previous March.

Letting Go of
Ownership of Content and Process

Sheila had been discovering that letting go of total ownership of a classroom was the way to walk through her fear of not being a "good teacher." The process of creating a cooperative-learning situation, however, was a struggle against her own habits:

> See, when you're there I'm reminded I need to move people
> so they can hear each other think. So sometimes I remember
> to do it. Like they even knew when we're gonna make this
> move. Sometimes I remember to do it and sometimes I really
> don't.
>   They should have moved their bodies so that they were
> talking to each other. That was good.

Even though the work of setting up the environment for this kind
of interaction was new for Sheila, her basic commitment to allowing
the students the freedom of their own ideas was never an issue. In
the March 31, 1989, interview she understood that having students
confront controversial issues put her at risk of a parent phone call.
She said, "I'm willing to take that risk," but she felt that that position
made her, as she said, "different from a lot of other teachers." Other
differences were not so easy to accept. In April 1989, Sheila offered
tentatively, "This semester the kids have done some really interesting
things, and I think that I'm being influenced to take more risks and
not really care if Ralph thinks . . ."

That spring as well she was beginning to accept that students at
VCRHS would not—and should not be expected to—be giving her
the affirmations that she had so loved at her previous school: "Number one, they can't do it. They don't know how to do it. And number
two, that's not why we're here."

As of May 16, 1989, she saw that students telling her how great
she was had an opposite side: They made her responsible for their
bad grades or other consequences of their own actions. The connection of one kind of emotional distance with the other made sense to
her as she heard herself describe to me an interaction with a student
who had said, "I'm suspended because of you."

> I said, "It's not because of me. It's because of you." And I
> believed that. I'm not agonizing over it. I would have, in the
> past. And that is too tiring. So I've given up one thing for the
> other.

Still, at the end of August 1989 in a phone conversation, she was
struggling again to figure out an appropriate balance in the relationship she established with her students:

The person I am is why I teach this way. . . . I *want* kids to
know who I am. Teachers model life. My personality is that
I'm accessible.

I'm willing to check in and call people up. I worry sometimes that I'm too accessible, because I think it hurts my
credibility.

The credibility she longed for had to do with the traditional role
of high school teachers, impressive in their very inaccessibility.
Therefore, moving herself away from center stage had an immediate
effect on her own view of herself. Sheila realized in June 1989 that
before the work of that year, she had been teaching by the force of
her personality, rather than by clearly setting goals and thinking
through how to achieve them:

I just thought, "We're gonna do these things. It'll be fun." I
didn't really think about what they would learn, necessarily.
I just wanted them to experience a whole bunch of different
things.

So I learned a lot of things about how to think about
school that I didn't think about before. I just did stuff. I was
a real spontaneous teacher.

This year I think my kids think they've learned things.
They've had to learn about what they think, and in the past
kids looked into what *I* thought, and they liked that.

I had a kid write me a note once that said, "Miss M., you
know everything," but she knew nothing. She wasn't ever
thinking about herself or what she thought at all, and I was
liking that she thought I knew everything. I was too busy
liking that.

I see them completely differently than in the past.
There's some way they had some connection to me, like they
were a part of me. Now I see them as themselves, and I can
be proud of where they are and let them have that pride, let
them own it. I don't have to own it.

Sheila had decided by July 1, 1989, that one of the things she
wanted to work on the next year would be the development of student responsibility by making time for people in groups to be able to

say to one another, "I did all the work today, you guys, and I don't like that." Understanding that the imbalance of responsibility was the chief reason students disliked being in small groups, she was looking forward to taking that step toward improvement of cooperation. In her statement of confidence in her ability to do that, it is possible to hear a prefiguring of what was to trouble her so much the next fall—the fact that she never got around to helping students master those social skills:

> I really feel confident I'm good at working with kids on their relationships with one another.
>
> A lot of times I think I shouldn't be teaching English. I should be doing some sort of—I don't know—interpersonal stuff, something. That's what I'm good at.
>
> I think it's worth a try to look at, have them process their own work in the group and struggle with that, because it's going to be very uncomfortable for them.
>
> It's not uncomfortable for me. It doesn't bother me to have kids talk about how they feel or to be angry. That's OK.
>
> One of the things I want them to know is you don't have to like each other to work well in a group. What you do is you have to respect each other. Everyone will have something to offer the group. No one should be a parasite, and how can we keep these things from happening?
>
> "What are you going to do? Make a list and I'll come back and help you with it, but you figure it out." Because that's life, isn't it, Liz? (July 1, 1989)

Although feeling she had to "prepare" students for what they would face next was still an issue for Sheila in November of 1989, she was struggling even then to claim the value for students of a fully student-centered approach as a legitimate alternative to traditional approaches to that preparation. From a former colleague whose work was very much like her own, Sheila got excited by the radical idea of giving up a book halfway through. She had the courage to implement the idea although her discussion of it with me sounded as if she was working on convincing herself that what she was doing was good educational practice:

Whatever happens with *The Heart Is a Lonely Hunter* (McCullers, 1967) is what's going to happen, and I'm going to start on Monday and I'm just going to see where we go with it.

And if we decide halfway through the book we're done, we want to stop reading it, that's what we'll do. . . . That's the way I'm going to do it because that makes sense to me. . . . I have to do what is going to be good for the class.

I need to be the kind of teacher that I know that I am. I don't even think of myself as a teacher when I think of myself that way. I just think of myself as a person engaged in learning with my students.

I sometimes make a lot of mistakes. Sometimes I do things really right. So when kids are done they think "Wow! I really did this! This is great! I get something!"

I really had fun today and I was thinking, isn't this funny? When I just back off, they're working happily along and I'm happy and we're not like creating any literary masterpieces, but so what? They just did it. But I didn't really bother them. If they wanted my help they asked for it. But they were just working on it.

It's kind of funny, how I feel—when I back off they— they—I think they feel that it's OK to do it their own way, I guess is what I'm saying.

How Should Students Read?

The difference between Ralph and Sheila on the issue of literary versus personal response to literature was something he acknowledged in September of 1989. Neither of them, however, anticipated how pivotal a difference it would become during their collaboration. In describing one of their early team-taught classes, in which he and Sheila had shared their own response papers to model what they were asking their students to do, Ralph said:

I think what they found out is that they were asking the same questions that *we* were, which was interesting. The second thing that they found out is that people respond in different ways. Sheila responded quite differently than how I responded, except in basic ideas that we all could agree on.

Sheila tended to approach it from the feminist point of view, which was of interest to her, and also from the theme and development of theme.

I tended to approach it in relation to works that I have been teaching at the 12th-grade level: to *Doctor Faustus* (Marlowe, 1604/1962), *Romeo and Juliet*—so I was making connection with other works and how the theme was being carried through and how it reminded me of those themes.

Also, I tended to respond to it in the development of allegory and the use of language, which tended to be my interest.

In spite of Sheila's conviction that reader response was better preparation for students' independent engagement with a piece of literature than the traditional literary criticism approach—collecting information for plot, character, setting, theme—the pull of Ralph's authority made her feel that she was "supposed to do it that way" (November 13, 1990). Whereas in our September conversation Ralph had expressed interest in what the students could come up with on their own, when I interviewed him again on November 13 he was talking about giving students guidelines: "These are important points you need to think about." Sheila still trusted that the students could generate their own "important points."

By September 1989, Sheila was working to talk less, engage less, and give the discussion over to the students, especially when there were several groups all reading different books. But Ralph was saying, "I have a feeling I'm going to be very lonely in there." Sheila had been at that stage of loneliness, of feeling left out and missing the conversation, many months before. She had dealt with her tendency to jump in, to fill up the silence, and to dominate the talk. Now she saw herself facilitating students' talking to one another. Ralph had not yet figured out how to share in the pleasure of intellectual exchange without being directly involved. He said:

In the great books class, I guess I had a vision of discussing what the philosophies are, about literature, about the great thinkers, or what makes a certain writer important, or that kind of thing. By each being individuals (and reading different books) that doesn't happen, and I can't generate a discussion. (November 13, 1989)

In his role as chair apart from classroom teacher, however, Ralph noted that some of the other members of his department were even less comfortable than he was with the change. His strategy with the teachers was to let them discover for themselves what the meaning of their own discomfort was:

> It's the one person that's had a problem all along with the power struggle between students and teachers. She feels very much the need to control. And what she has done is she's outlined everything for them, exactly what they're to know and so forth.
>
> The consequences have been interesting, though. Out of her class—she started with 15 students—I had a request from three students to drop. . . . And at this point we're just letting them change. Hopefully what will happen is that at the end of the quarter the teacher will realize that there's no one in the class except those students who like to memorize.

He was not yet willing to give that kind of discovery learning over to his students.

The difference that emerged out of the daily contact between Ralph and Sheila was that Sheila was talking primarily about process, and Ralph, in terms of his classroom at least, was saying very clearly that his interest was end products. The issue became that of having the seniors do a formal paper. Ralph's view was that the formal paper was of primary significance. Sheila was more concerned, in mid-October 1989, with what she perceived as the students not really sharing once they had "collected information." She said,

> To me, the formal paper is just one piece. But I really start to feel I'm not on the right track. Ralph says his groups are fantastic, and mine are not. I have a lot of anxiety. This morning, I had mega anxiety: What if they're right and I'm wrong?

Even if the other teachers were right and she was wrong, a further anxiety was that she felt she did not know how to do it well, either way. Ralph was giving worksheets to students in his section of their course (November 12, 1989), but Sheila said,

I don't know if I can decide what the kids need to know when they compare. His framework doesn't make sense to me. I would like *them* to define the framework. But they can't, yet—when they get together and talk about the book, they don't *do* anything.

I'm not sure what they're *supposed* to be doing in their groups. The way the course was set up made group work really hard. If I could slow it down—they could work with one other person, instead of large groups.

Distance Versus Engagement

It was December 1, 1989, when Sheila said to me in both despair and resignation, "I think the people I work with are very traditional teachers." She meant that even if sometimes students talked with one another in their classrooms, most of the teachers were and seemed comfortable with remaining content-centered and teacher-centered. If the use of groups was a surface change rather than a deep change, her professional values were not fully shared. Once she could name that, it seemed that she could think about separating herself from the choices other teachers made and focus on meeting her own standards. Living there daily was not easy for her:

I just feel like we're really different, and I know that they hired me because of those differences that I now feel sort of penalized for. I feel sort of penalized. Someone said to me after a faculty meeting, "Oh, you always rock the boat. Why don't you just shut up?"

She had thought a lot about just shutting up from early into her first year at VCRHS. As soon as she began to see that her style of directly engaging in difficult issues was not the norm and that her concerns were not the same as those expressed by most of the rest of the faculty, she realized that it would be a lot easier not to say what was on her mind, especially outside of the classroom. But it was inconsistent with her vision for her to retreat into the safety of the distancing academic posture, and it troubled her that so many of her colleagues seemed to do that.

The students were aware of the differences between Sheila and traditional teachers. They characterized one of the differences in physical terms, both metaphorically and actually:

First Student She really gets around to see us. She makes a point of that every single day.

Liz And you feel she knows you pretty well? She's not off in her judgments?

First Student No.

Second Student For someone to be able to, you heard her in class today. She knows exactly what everybody is reading. She knows where they are.

Third Student Unlike some teachers, they just like stand up there and they teach, but they're standing far away.

Second Student They're teaching everybody, not just you.

Third Student Yeah, and you're just supposed to take it in, and stuff.

Fourth Student And if you don't, you don't.

Second Student If you need help or something, she's not somebody you're afraid to ask. (December, 1989)

As early chapters indicate, Sheila worked most carefully to make the classroom exactly the kind of safe space the students were describing. She was giving students choices. She was managing the classroom in such a way that she didn't have to be combative with students or have them be in competition with one another. She thought carefully about whether or not it would be useful to give a grade each time there was a set of papers. Usually, she just wrote comments, often personal response comments, especially on drafts. Students reported to me that they really appreciated how she read their papers. They felt that she really heard them.

When the focus was on the students' proving that they knew the content, there was no room for their dealing with text beyond a surface level. Proving knowledge was what Sheila rejected, for both herself and her students. She did not want to be "the expert": "I could care less if kids think I know everything. I *don't* know everything. I don't even want to *claim* to know everything" (December, 1989).

Nor did she want her students to have to try to be experts, or at least "get it right," in order to get a top grade. It troubled her that grades seemed to be the focus at VCRHS:

> [The school] is not really committed to having kids think
> about things: It's having them get the right answers. And I
> think this is what some teachers despise about me, is that I
> don't know what the right answer is for interpretation of
> literature. (December, 1989)

Whatever it might mean for traditional teachers to be "prepared"
for a class, for Sheila it meant "having a comfort level when we do a
book together, so I can be as aware as [the students] are, so I know
how far to push something. I usually review the night before."

She would not be satisfied with having students merely "collect
information" for themselves any more than she was with having
them attend to a teacher who had collected information for them and
was telling them how to think about it. Her aim was on a different
level: "When you have the information, what are you going to *do* with
it? . . . You collect the information and then you take an *action* on the
information" (January 7, 1989).

Giving Up the Need for Approval

At the very least, if they could not be models or even allies for
her, Sheila had not expected her colleagues to undermine her teaching. But that was what she felt was sometimes happening. It got so
that small interactions took on almost symbolic power. Although she
did not yet feel she could directly say anything about her discomfort
to the teacher in whose room she taught the first year, that teacher's
frequent coming in to water her plants or shuffle papers during
Sheila's class felt like a devaluing of the work that was going on,
however informal the classroom interactions appeared.

If Sheila had felt confident enough about her teaching, she would
have spoken to the teacher and they would have understood one
another. In fact, if she had felt confident, she would not have minded
anyone's coming and going, especially during the time when small
groups were comfortably buzzing. But Sheila felt her position in the
building to be so precarious, she did not dare ask for the freedom she
needed from even that much exposure.

What Sheila was experiencing as reactions from her colleagues
was quite predictable according to the research, as was suggested in
Chapter 1. But Sheila did not have the benefit of a wider vantage

point to buoy her up when she started working at VCRHS. Even if she had, her original expectations of her colleagues had been that they too would be actively engaged in "innovative teaching methods" (August, 1990). So she questioned herself, especially when things weren't working in the classroom as she had expected them to work. She said, "Ralph gives little quizzes, and it's funny, with my juniors, sometimes I feel like I should do that, because I know some don't read" (March 31, 1989).

That was her own disapproval of herself. What she also saw was active disapproval by other teachers of the ways that did work for her:

> Those are the kinds of stories I tell because they make sense to kids. Kids understand that. They know what it would feel like to be left out of things. But I don't think the other teachers like that I do that. I'm positive that they don't, because they have criticized that in other people. (March 31, 1989)

In the midst of a long section of our conversation in which she described the wonderful work her students were doing, she interrupted herself to say: "I'm worried that when they go to somebody else, they'll be asked to trace the plot line, and they won't be able to do that" (May 9, 1989).

What Sheila ultimately did to protect herself from becoming debilitated by the disapproval of her colleagues was to stop talking with them about what she was doing in her classroom. On December 30, 1989, she said to me on the phone: "I need to hang around with people who believe what I do is right—kids making all the connections themselves, not me telling them 'the answers.' "

"Easy"

Sheila felt like an outcast at VCRHS during the 1988-1989 school year. Frequently she would say during that year, especially that fall, "It would just be easier to do it their way," "Maybe I should . . .," "I would just like to fit in," and "I don't know." Her doubts magnified in the fall of 1989 during the close collaboration she and Ralph had decided to do with their senior classes. Early in August before the school year started, she wrote in her journal that she was already having anxiety dreams about school.

Although she was eager to try out the exciting things they had planned together and she had felt a complete mutuality in that planning, her anxiety seemed to increase with the chronic worry, "Will I be good enough?" This time her interactions and her choices would be under the daily scrutiny of her chair as well as subjected to my regular intrusion on her autonomy. With regard to me, she was afraid she would let me down. The fear was more immediate with Ralph. As soon as the semester started, he began to criticize their class of seniors, all of whom had been with her as juniors. As early as September 6, 1989, her journal cries out, "He says their writing skills are weak! Should I take responsibility? Kids aren't prepared! This makes me crazy!"

She was very hard on herself that first week of school in 1989, knowing that she wasn't living up to her professional ideals for herself:

> I talk too much. I say and tell too many answers. I don't know how to set it up so *they* do the work. I don't know how to set up the class so I am less important and they are the most important.
>
> I want them to believe I am a good teacher. Sometimes their approval is really important to me. This is tiresome.
>
> I talk too much and have a reputation for it. . . . I feel like a terrible teacher, like I can't get it right, like I make too many mistakes. Is it true in other professions that people feel so inadequate? Some days I feel like I'll never get it right.

Within 2 weeks, an issue arose that escalated her doubts about herself. Teachers, especially Ralph, began telling her that the students thought she was easy. The suggestion was that the teachers also thought so, implying that an easy teacher is not a good teacher. How could she understand what was meant by "easy," and what should she do about it? She took it as deep criticism. Was she not rigorous? Did the students not work as hard in her classes as they were expected to in other classes? Was it true? Was it bad? She tried to think it through in her journal: "Sometimes I feel outraged that my classes are perceived as ways out for kids. Is it so bad for a kid to feel good in a class? Does that mean they aren't working or learning?"

By October 1, 1989, Sheila's confusion had intensified. Ralph was still continually saying that the seniors she had taught the year before "can't write; they have no skills." She took his criticism as a personal attack on her teaching and was feeling terribly vulnerable. What if it was true? In a phone call, she directly asked me for help of the sort that I could give:

> It would be helpful for you to observe other teachers at Valley Central so I can test my perceptions. Maybe I'm doing it wrong. It comes back to me that I'm not giving [kids] anything. The way *I* do it, when they're on to something, I say, "I think you're on to something."
>
> I think—I don't know—I get nervous. What I think I want them to do when they read is think about what's going on in the story, starting with themselves.
>
> Sometimes I feel uncomfortable, because [the students] feel they're not *getting* anything. I can live with it, but it makes me very nervous.
>
> I want kids to feel challenged, stretched, but without pressure. They feel it's easy. They say, "I can relax." Maybe they should be scared and nervous like they are with other teachers.
>
> It's not helpful to compare myself to others, but I care about how they perceive me. And I really care about how the kids see what they're learning. Ralph is already saying to me that I'm too easy. I felt defensive. I need for someone whose ego is not involved to give me feedback. The sooner you could come, the better.

Ten days later, Sheila was writing similarly despairing thoughts in her journal:

> Someone walked into my 12th-grade class and said [the kids were all in groups, talking loudly, excitedly, about books they were reading]: "*What a zoo!*" I take these comments to heart, and I wonder whether or not it *is* a zoo?

On October 12, she again expressed the contradiction she felt. Even though she had evidence that students could learn in new ways and could even learn to be cooperative in a competitive society, she wondered if she was doing them a disservice. Should she disengage from constantly comparing herself to others, which was such a disabling direction for her? Should she, for the students' sake, do it the "regular" way? Her self-doubt, as expressed in that journal entry, was extremely painful:

> Can the old ways still work in new times? Can we say that having all students together is really beneficial? Can we say that in not giving them the answers they will find their own way? Was I barely functioning last year to teach kids? Did they learn anything? Why do they seem so regressed this year? Why does it matter so desperately what kids think? Can I trust myself? Can I believe that what I do is good and right? Will "they" tell us in 10 years that all of this is BS, that it doesn't work this way, that we should do it like it was done in the beginning? I'm scared that because I don't project myself as the expert, that I end up having no credibility. I doubt myself and my intelligence.
>
> And perhaps I must be satisfied to be a lonely voice, a lone voice, a different voice . . . in a different voice.

The broader perspective from Gilligan (1982) in that repetition may have been her comfort for right then. Four days later, I sat in as Sheila and Ralph "debriefed" about the course they were teaching together. They spoke about an English department meeting in which Sheila had felt criticized by some colleagues for using the reader-response notebook. The other English teachers were saying that reader response did not work for them; that is, it did not get at the knowledge they wanted the students to gain. Sheila heard an implicit criticism of the method. Again, she felt personally attacked: "What I felt was that I really believe in my heart that the response notebook is a tool, it's a good tool. But if it's misused it won't be as successful" (October 16, 1989).

Still feeling shaky, she tried to check out her perceptions with Ralph. She had taken the risk of sharing her students' response notebooks with the department, fully expecting that everyone else would see as she did that they were beautiful products. It troubled her deeply that "they didn't appreciate them." It was hard for her to confront directly the reality that what she valued was not valued by her colleagues: "What I was concerned about was if my perceptions or my expectations are different, then—I was just concerned about it."

Days after my visit, she told me on the phone of the seniors she and Ralph were teaching together and whom he thought of as unprepared,

> When these kids came to me [as juniors], they all wrote the same thing. My goal is to have them engaged. If that's my goal, then I'm successful. If my goal is to prepare them for something else, I'm not successful.
>
> I value the product, too, but the *way* they do that is more important than what they end up with.

She could see that other people in the department were trying very hard to act on their decision to practice cooperative learning as they understood it. She also knew that she was still so new at it that she could not provide them the support she knew they needed. Just after our cooperative-learning workshop, Sheila had spoken with admiration of Sally, the member of the English department who had had the most years of teaching: "I'm not sure she knows what to do with this group thing, but she really thinks a lot about it, and she's trying to figure out a way to have it be different" (April 25, 1989).

Sheila understood objectively that the others in the department were probably venting on her the frustration they were feeling when things that were so unfamiliar did not seem to go well in their classrooms. But it did not seem fair. She was vulnerable enough to feel "stupid" because the other English teachers

> already know what they want the kids to find, . . . and I don't always know what I want them to find. It gets confusing. I get confused about what my job is. I told my class how well they're doing, and Ralph said, "Don't tell them." (April 25, 1989)

Mothering

Sheila felt most deeply accused around the issue of her close relationship with the students. It confused and hurt her when Ralph started saying that she was being like a mother with them. She heard a clear implication that in his conception of the role of teacher, "mothering" was inappropriate. For his part, he told her that he refused to be their parent; he was not going to hold their hands. His statements again made her very defensive because she cherished the nurturing she did in the classroom. Her accessibility to them was what she felt made the space safe for them to grow. She recognized that she was asking students to do risky work, academically and socially. Thus, she felt it was her job to be there alongside them as they did that work, encouraging them, believing in them, knowing when to nag them and when to leave them alone, and supporting them until they were sure enough to do it completely without her. Was that holding their hands? If so, why was hand-holding inappropriate in a high school?

The confusing relationship with both Ralph and her other colleagues in the department made Sheila so doubt her perceptions of her own teaching that she felt personally vulnerable to the criticism she heard in reaction to her teaching methods. During my October 1989 visit to the school, I listened while Sheila and Ralph talked about the recent department meeting. He was trying to affirm how hard the mandated change toward heterogeneous grouping and cooperative learning felt to everyone in the department. She would acknowledge that because it was also very difficult for her, but she wanted some recognition for what was, in fact, going on in the transforming classrooms:

Sheila I would balk at a kid saying we're not *doing* anything. We're doing an *enormous* amount of work!

Ralph Teachers perceive other teachers as doing nothing because they're not doing what *they* do. Even *I* used to think that way. It's part of not knowing, of never knowing what each other does. . . . Your perception of the tone at the meeting—we were exploring, but you thought we were criticizing you. It's easier for you to do group work. You're younger. We buy into it when we see it work.

But what was it about Sheila that made her "buy into it" without having seen it work? And if she was the only one doing it, how could she not take their comments personally, especially when it was true, even after so much effort and time, that much of what she wanted to do wasn't quite working yet for her either? The difference seemed to be that Sheila was willing to struggle until it did work, perhaps because she believed that it could:

It was like, oh, god, well, what if they *aren't* reading? Maybe I should give quizzes. And then I thought, I can have them— if I'm worried about them there are things I can do in terms of writing.

Their notebooks certainly serve as one indicator. I don't know. It was just kind of funny. It was a weird feeling.

By November 5, 1989, all of the criticism had begun to exhaust Sheila. What she told me on the phone sounded very much like what she had said the year before: "I really feel like I run the risk of becoming like the other people in the building, just to survive—give up the struggle, look the other way. I said to Ralph, 'This is too hard.' "

When I went back to the school on November 13, Sheila had gone deeper into herself about the difference between what she was asking of her students as readers and what the other members of the department were asking:

> I'm really scared. I'm scared, but I'm not giving them the guidelines, but I think they can say, "OK, let's look at the character . . ." That's what I think is the reason why we read, and why we teach English, teach literature to kids. I understand, however, that that is not why other people teach it.
>
> And so that's my dilemma, because I don't want them to not be prepared to be literary, but I want them to engage as a human being with a novel that is presenting other human beings' lives.

"I Thought I Had to"

By the time she wrote in her journal on October 17, 1989, Sheila was ready to cave in. The handwriting in that entry is tight and small, compared to the wild, swift, exploring, wide-ranging writing of the earlier entries. The lines look like a poem—determined, almost careful, and desperately sad:

> I have decided that I am *not* a good teacher.
>> The top students don't like me.
>> They don't like groups.
>> They don't like heterogeneous groups.

They want to have Ralph lead them in great philosophical discussion.

I feel ignorant and unable to get a class to do the kind of thinking that he can get them to do—I wish I could be more like Ralph.

I am so worried about being a bad teacher.

I want kids to think I'm good and smart—what I think happens is that kids think I'm nice—but don't really learn much from me.

This feels shitty.

Sheila told me on the phone (November 8, 1989) that she felt Ralph was blaming her "for our students not doing better." Now the issue was not just their writing skills but that they "can't analyze a novel":

He blames me, and *I* blame me. . . . I'm so confused. I feel he's telling me I have to do it his way or they won't learn anything. . . . I feel he's saying if I'm not like him I'm no good. . . . I feel really bad—I had expected I would work with Ralph and with these kids. Kids say, "You'll learn so much from him because he knows everything."

So she began to require her students to do a formal essay and to spend their groups collecting information on plot, character, setting, and theme. But she was not happy: "I'm so frustrated, I sent a résumé somewhere, and they're not schools" (November 11, 1989).

Nor were the students happy. When I visited on November 10, she described the changes:

Sheila I haven't been fun with the seniors. I've been all businesslike, and they're not used to that. . . . So today I just relaxed with them. I think it was like everyone was breathing a sigh of relief.

Liz "She's back."

Sheila Yeah, and they've known it. They even said to me, "You're becoming just like him."

She could know that, but 2 days later my intervention helped her catch herself about to make photocopies for her class of a worksheet that Ralph had designed for a book that his class was reading but hers was not.

The faculty's dominant attitude of mistrusting students was also affecting her. A week after my visit, she told me on the phone that she was afraid of using my suggestion that she put students into stage one jigsaw groups (Aronson, 1978)—checking in with others who had the same assignment to make sure they felt prepared—before taking on the teaching task of the stage two jigsaw groups. Her fear was that students would just hitchhike.

She saw only that outcome, which was of course possible. Because she was being drawn into the traditional mind-set about student laziness, she did not look at the other, positive outcomes that normally she would have been the first to see: (a) that hitchhikers would at least have to perform in their second stage groups; (b) that they would discover what it feels like when peers care to find out what you think and how you back it up; and (c) that with the preliminary step, individuals become "experts" partly by having the chance to check their perceptions with others, so careless reasoning does not go unchecked.

She understood intellectually that scuttling the first step allows the teacher to know who did the work and who did not, but it shortchanges the process of student thinking. Clearly her colleagues' traditional deep mistrust of students "getting away with something" was affecting her professional judgment.

As of a phone conversation on December 17, 1989, she was still thinking about giving up teaching because she felt her integrity had been challenged, and she had her limits:

> I'm worried that I'm becoming like the other teachers, focusing on unimportant things because that's what *they're* interested in. When I got together with my friend Sharon, I realized how far I've moved from my own vision of teaching. It scares me.
>
> I let them define me, and that's making me nuts. I'm discouraged by how I've succumbed to the pressure of the group. I don't feel I have enough touch with people who are doing right in their teaching. . . . I have the fear I'll become like the place where I work.

I want to be accepted. I'm tired of being *out* there, all by myself. I want to fit in. That means I'll have to compromise. That may mean I have to leave the profession.

I have to live with the criticism, and I don't know if I'm strong enough. I don't want to be working *against*. It's really tiring. But I haven't succumbed to interpreting literature for kids.

Nor did she succumb to total despair. When I visited her at the school the next day (December 18, 1989), she was already understanding that what she had done in becoming someone other than herself had not been right for kids, and she was deciding to reclaim her own way:

Sheila   I can redeem next semester. I mean, I can look forward to that and say, OK, what I really started to do, that's what— OK, what is the most important thing to me? The most important thing to me is to have them begin to talk to one another, so how am I going to set that up? If that's my goal, how will I set that up? And I can do that. I know how to do it. So that's what I want to focus on, instead of worrying that when they go to another teacher their skills won't be good enough and they'll be punished and I'll be punished. . . . I felt like this year I had betrayed them.

Liz   By making them do the formal essay or by not having prepared them?

Sheila   By making them do it.

Liz   So let me ask this. Why did you cave in and do it?

Sheila   Because I'm scared, because I was worried, and I thought I was supposed to.

The Need for Positive Feedback

What Sheila had needed all along was validation: "I really thought what my students were doing was good, but sometimes I'm just not sure. Like I would like for someone else to say, 'This is good' " (November 4, 1989).

In particular, that "someone else" from whom she needed affirmation was Ralph. But maybe he could not give it: "He should be boosting me up, because he's the chair, but I don't think he can, because he's struggling with it himself" (November 4, 1989).

By our mid-November conversations, however, Sheila was beginning to accept two things: (a) that it was not Ralph's way to give praise and (b) that he was beginning to do some things her way in his own classroom, after watching her. That imitation might have to be enough affirmation for her.

She was beginning to claim her own ways of doing things, even though they were very different from his ways, but she was still afraid of Ralph's saying of yet another class that she was not giving them what they needed. She could not handle that criticism because part of her believed it was true.

At the end of that month, she was telling me on the phone that she had decided what she needed:

> The less I talk with other people, the better. I don't want to engage with them—it keeps me sane. I'm avoiding setting myself up. I'm not going to feed into their negativity about the kids.
>
> It would be really helpful if I had other people observing me.

All this time, however, it didn't occur to her to ask Ernest to be that supportive observer. When I came to visit on December 1, part of her was still tied in to the agenda set by traditional teachers:

> I thought, this is really good. So I don't know. But I mean, if one of *them* were watching the lesson, I'm not sure they would see it that way. I always think, well, I should teach grammar, and why aren't I teaching grammar? I just don't think it's that important. What I've read is that you have to use students' own writing to teach grammar.

> **Liz** So then why do you think you should be teaching grammar?
> **Sheila** Well, because *they're* doing it (laughs). Kids like doing those exercises. They really think that's learning something.

There seemed to be no one in the building who was prepared to give positive feedback on the kind of teaching that valued such skills as learning to listen. As Sheila saw it, people seemed to be talking only about how great their own classes were. That was not helpful to a teacher who knew that her own classes were in process but not yet "great." For the first year and a half, she allowed herself to be intimidated by their talk. Then, out of her own need to distance herself from caring about what they said, she had begun to look at the realities and the feelings behind those postures. She also began to realize that the way the institution of schooling is set up, other teachers also needed but never got what she knew she needed but never got: "We're desperate for someone to say, 'You're doing a really good job,' because no one does" (March 5, 1990).

Ironically, once she started letting go of expecting encouragement for her work within the building, Sheila began to be aware that there might be unspoken support, though not in the way she had wished for it to appear. She told me in mid-December about a department meeting in which she had longed for someone to stand up with her in public. After the meeting, Jane, another English teacher, had quietly let her know that she agreed with the stands Sheila was taking, and that she was also experimenting with the methods that Sheila was describing. Another source of support was my summary of her students' conversations with me that same week. From that she could hear that she was getting through to students with what she cared about, including having them feel that they would be well prepared for wherever they were going next.

It was obvious to both of us, however, that she was distressed, and that she was distancing from both her former self and her students. She was deliberately forgetting about teaching as relationship. The students had noticed and let her know. Some were frankly angry about her having turned traditional on them. Others saw perhaps more. Sheila reported that one student told her with some hostility as well as concern: "You don't smile as much this year." Sheila knew what the cause was: "I'm painfully aware of his [Ralph's] disapproval." It was hard for her to separate her teaching from her identity and not to take the criticism personally. But by early December 1989, she was beginning to work on herself about that: "What I've been thinking is that if you need to speak on this issue or you need to do things a certain way, then accept that people aren't going to like it. That's a given, and you keep going."

She told me on the phone in mid-December that one of the things that helped her was hearing herself back on the tape of one of our

conversations. "I have to own what I am," she said. But it was not
going to be easy:

> I've been trying to change to be like other people. It would
> be easier. Sometimes I get tired. I want the conflict to be over.
> I always use other people as my point of reference, but some-
> times those people aren't the best choices for me. They don't
> value what I value.

In another phone call at the end of December, she said, "I let them
[other faculty] set the terms if I care about or worry about whether
they like me. I have to learn not to do that."

She was still reacting in early January to the pressure of how
other people were doing things:

> I think Valley Central is making me feel like I ought to be a
> certain way, and I think I've been really influenced by that. I
> mean in [the previous teaching job], no one really cared
> about those kids.
>
>   So I didn't feel pressure. I only felt pressure to my stu-
> dents. I felt responsible for them, to make them feel good.
> That was my priority.
>
>   Here, I've been phobic about skills. But there, I didn't
> open a grammar book once in 2 years. But they gained con-
> fidence that they could do things, and that was really impor-
> tant to me.
>
>   Now I feel like I'm supposed to be doing all this other
> stuff and preparing them for this test. . . . I mean I never really
> thought about that before. And then I didn't lose my confi-
> dence. I think when you lose your confidence, forget it.

At the end of January 1990, however, there was a different tone
in Sheila's description of how she perceived things:

> When kids around here say I'm "easy," I really am coming
> to believe that what they mean is that I'm easy to be with . . .

that I listen to what they say. They probably don't think that anything great is happening to them. But I see that it is.

Once she had decided for herself that "easy" meant "the pressure is off," she could accept being different from Ralph:

> They're not doing worksheets . . . like Ralph's class, but that's OK. It's really OK. How they perceive it is going to be second to how I perceive it. He faults me for that. He said, "Kids think you're easy, and you don't give them worksheets like I do."
> And I said, "You're right. I'm going to give them directions on how I want them to go about reading something, and for some of the 9th graders I might have to give them directed questions, because they might struggle a lot with comprehension. Besides that, that's all I need to do. They can do the rest of the work themselves, and if they think that that makes my class easier, that's fine. That's all well and good. That's the way that it goes." (January, 1990)

After that late January conversation, I heard only occasional references to how other people did things or how they reacted to Sheila's doing things. She appeared to have let go of needing the approval of others—any others. Certainly she had let go of what had almost been an obsession with peer approval, almost since the beginning of her teaching at VCRHS, but increasingly during her semester of team-teaching with Ralph. She expressed occasional worry about how her choices would be perceived, but mainly our conversations looked closely at whatever she was working on at the time in her particular classrooms. These conversations were fewer in number than during the fall semester of 1989 when she had initiated phone calls and extra meetings. With regard to Ralph, by the end of April 1990, she had come to terms with the difference in their approaches: "He and I are a good balance, because he will *give* them all of that, and I guess for some of them they *need* it. But they will get it from him. I'm not worried."

By June 1990, she had decided to take the course he was offering at the university, because she knew there was still a lot she could learn from him.

Reclaiming What She Knew

December of 1989 had been a very low point for Sheila. She felt overwhelmed by the contradictions between what she'd been led to believe other teachers were doing and what she found them actually doing. She was tired of the struggle, feeling that she had so little "resistance to people's behaviors" right then:

> **Sheila** I know if they cut my job at the end of the year I wouldn't look for another teaching job, Liz. I know it. I just feel like I couldn't. I don't know how long I can do it. I worry about that because I feel that I—I think that if I were stronger, I could do it.
>
> **Liz** What do you mean by "stronger"?
>
> **Sheila** If I could really say to myself, and believe, that what I do is fine. It might not be the best. It might not be the worst, but it's fine. This is the way I am. Instead of always fighting with myself. I think that's just the tiring part, actually, I don't know. I'm not really sure about what to do about that piece, 'cause I think that's the piece that needs the most. The other people aren't going to change. They're going to do things the way that they do them, and I'm the one that needs to say, "I don't want to be like them." So I have to—I have to accept me.

By May 1990, she had gotten there. In fact, she had begun to bounce back fast. By January 7, 1990, once she was again teaching on her own, she was on her way to claiming her own values, working toward them, and feeling that she wanted to:

> I would like a couple more years at VCRHS, because I feel like some of these things I want to try out and work on them a little more, just to see if in fact I believe they can work.

In the January 26 visit, 4 days into a new semester with a new set of classes, she was really happy: "They get it!" When I asked her about a certain group of three girls who sat in a line rather than face-to-face, she described her thinking:

> Well, Carol was one of the people that was having some trouble. I asked them if they would let her come work with them, and I figured let them do it the way that they want.
>
> Even if they don't talk to each other or include Carol, just sitting with them she's with the group. Let's just see how it goes for today.

Of another class I noticed, "Look at how comfortable they are!" She replied with pleasure:

> They're just really nice. See, that's what I find. I actually think that's my strong suit. I have to remember always to work from it: it's that I'm real easy for kids to be with. And so I can avoid any kind of conflict or ill feeling if I just work from that.
>
> I've decided that I have to do this my way. It's the only way I'll be happy about it. Whatever anyone else thinks, let them think it.

What had changed was her focus:

> I guess when I was busy worrying about whether Ralph was approving of me, I was kind of worrying about my relationship with him, instead of my relationship with my students, which is really what I'm good at.
>
> Like if I focus on how much I like them, even though I work hard, it's easy; it's fun! I have fun with them. But when I was worrying about that other stuff it made me so tense I felt like I wasn't really enjoying it as much. I do this 'cause I like *them*!

They appeared to know that. Even when they were almost unanimously not enjoying the group work, they trusted Sheila because they felt how much she cared for them. In fact, what may have been for her the most difficult part of knowing how Ralph disliked the senior class was not so much that she felt his criticism of them to be a direct criticism of her preparation of them, but that she *liked* them and she wanted others to appreciate them as she did.

By March 5, 1990, Sheila seemed to be sure of her choices as she separated herself cleanly from the role of traditional teacher: "What I realize is that even though I might want to change the persona, I can't. It doesn't work, because I want to enjoy the day. That's how I do it."

More often now she was planning to trust the students and her structuring of activities when she went into the classroom:

> I'm just going to play it by ear, actually. Like with my 10th grade, there's a bunch of different things I could do, but I'm just going to see what happens. So it might be that they spend most of the time writing, which would be OK. So I don't know. We'll see how it goes.

The description above sounds different from the unplanned spontaneity that she said characterized her early teaching, though clearly that early experience prefigured this one. This time what happened in a class would not depend on her alone, but she was feeling comfortable rather than terrified about that fact.

She still was saying "I don't know," but the tone was very different from the frequent "I don't know" that meant "I'm uncomfortable," "Maybe I'm not sure," or "I don't know how," which characterized the March 1989 dialogue (7 instances of "I don't know"), and especially the April 1989 dialogue (16 instances). In early May, "I don't know" appeared 8 times, but it was more than balanced by "maybe" (15 instances), as in "maybe we could." "Maybe" appeared frequently again in the mid-May interviews, in connection with "probably," "some possibilities," and "one way we could've done it . . ." Again on December 1, 1989, however, "I don't know" reappeared in the original, unsure tone (6 instances in 2 pages) and again in the January 7 dialogue (5 instances in 4 pages). In mid-February, she was saying "It's hard" 27 times in 41 pages! She was also saying, "So we just have to work at that." By the March 5, 1990, interview, she said "I don't know" or "I'm not sure yet" 8 times, with the "yet" signaling movement toward optimism. In the same interview, "That's interesting!" appears 9 times. She could wait:

I can shift around . . . I don't know. I'm not real sure yet. I'm going to wait and see what happens today. I do that a lot. I kind of wait and just feel out what the best thing might be.

For Sheila, the new semester's autonomy within her classes was partly responsible for her changed attitude. She had expected that would be so, and throughout the difficult fall semester she worked to remind herself that it would soon be over and she would get a chance to start anew, as herself:

I feel like I made a commitment . . . to having my class be the way I know that it can be, which is very comfortable, very easy, very happy, and not a lot of stress. Which I really think is very important for children.

Here on March 20, 1990, she was *claiming* the word "easy" that previously she had so despised.

Someone Else Is Trying
Student-Centered Teaching

Sometime during the difficult semester when Sheila was struggling against defining her own work in terms of how Ralph was teaching, she began to have conversations with Jacob, the seventh-grade science teacher, who got to school as early as she did in the mornings to use the photocopy machine. Except for their mutual need to run off copies, Jacob and Sheila would not have had an opportunity to talk, even though they worked at the same school. The difference in departments and in age levels that they taught meant that there was no time built into a school day or year for them even to discover how much they could share professionally. As it turned out, their ideas about teaching separated both of them from their peers, exaggerating the isolation of teachers that is especially characteristic of high schools (Lortie, 1975; Sarason, 1982).

What drew them to one another was that they both believed that students can construct the meanings within texts and experiences if the teacher takes the time to help them develop the skills with which to do so. For Sheila, Jacob was the first person she had found in the

building who did not have doubts about trusting kids that completely. Jacob's aim for his students was that they essentially behave
like scientists: identifying problems, collaborating on setting criteria
for making decisions, and then experimenting with options for solu-
tions, knowing that "not every problem is going to have an easy
solution to it" (March 5, 1990). He did not want his students to be
"constantly spitting back information on a knowledge level"; instead, he wanted them to "learn how to solve problems using each
other's ideas."

One of the frustrations that he brought to discuss with Sheila was
that his students

> don't know how to ask each other questions that are relevant
> to their study. . . . They know how to work in groups as far
> as completing the tasks. They say, "Tell me what to do and
> I'll do it." (March 5, 1990)

As Sheila had found, Jacob saw that students knew how to "collect
information" but needed practice in figuring out that they had to take
that information somewhere and do something with it. Like Sheila,
however, Jacob was willing to look at the struggle to get students to
think as a process for which he was willing to give time and energy,
moving back himself so that his role became watching and listening:
"So it's going to be interesting to see what they do."

Sheila and Jacob reinforced one another's belief that the process
of coming to understanding, not the reproduction of knowledge, was
what should go on in a classroom. In resisting the notion of a sacred
body of knowledge that students should "get," Jacob was playing
with ways to have them, instead, engage with texts in ways that were
relevant to their lives. Sheila found an ally in Jacob, who had been
essentially writing his own science materials since he started teaching in experiential ways. He talked to me about having presented to
his department a curriculum that "cut the content in half" because
he wanted to save time to "give kids an opportunity to process
ideas."

Jacob and Sheila probably collaborated most effectively as a direct function of being in different content areas. Because they were
not feeling bound by a common "canon," their conversations focused, as Jacob told me, on "kids, and learning, and our views of

how kids learn and what kinds of learning situations we'd like to create in our classrooms" (March 22, 1990).

Because of his contact with Sheila, Jacob felt that he was more conscious of and now had strategies for helping students to

> become a little bit more aware of what they're doing and why they're doing it, and why groups are important. . . . I began realizing that I needed to do more on giving them some tools to be able to evaluate their performance and how they share ideas.
>
> She gave me some stuff from Johnson and Johnson (1975). . . . She helped me with that, just getting that organized and helping me put that together.

Jacob was grateful for her help. For her part, Sheila had told me that she felt she was learning from him: "I think he's probably really good at group problem solving—better—I think that's something I can really learn from him, how you have a problem and you solve it as a group" (March 5, 1990).

Jacob did not feel, however, that he had already arrived at where he wanted to be with his classes. He saw himself still working to get there, seeing it as a process as Sheila did. Jacob was probably the only other person in the building who acknowledged to Sheila that he was in struggle. In the March 22 interview with me after I had observed two of his classes, he used that kind of language:

Jacob They don't understand that area that is between copying a paper and sharing ideas and happening to have the same information down and that's OK, as long as you're sharing. . . . So that's the stuff I'm struggling with the kids that they've never learned. Maybe that's too much. I don't know.

Liz Does it feel like too much?

Jacob (Pause) Um, some days it does. Some days it feels like they should be able to—it feels like I'm really wondering if this is maybe expecting too much. Maybe I need to break down the steps more. . . . My job now is to work with them individually and to work more as a facilitator. . . . They are very careful not to criticize each other's work. It's a real problem. . . . They don't know how to challenge each other's thinking.

Liz Without challenging the person.

Jacob Right, without challenging personally. And some people
say that kids that age can't do that, but I disagree. I disagree.
I think kids can *do* that, but they need a model for doing that.

Sheila admired Jacob for his focus on his students rather than on
getting across a body of knowledge (April 22, 1990). Clearly, his sense
of his role as a teacher seemed to be, like Sheila's, different from that
of most of the other teachers in the building. Consequently, the two
of them also shared a sense of themselves as outcasts, alienated from
most of the other teachers in the building. But when I asked Jacob
(March 22, 1990) whether he had felt some pressure to "do more
content because that's what the 8th-grade curriculum is," he had
found his support in research:

Not at all. If anything, I've realized that what I'm doing is
right on the money. When I read the new College Board recommendations about secondary science, when I looked at
American Association for the Advancement of Science Foundation, and I looked at the new national recommendations
from the National Science Teachers Association, I realized
that what I've been doing for the last 5 or 6 years is right on
the money and that what other people are doing is a disservice to kids.

He was also spending time in elementary school classrooms, watching excellent group work in some of them. So he had seen the process
function, and that gave him support. Time spent in elementary classrooms reinforced the view that he and Sheila shared: A classroom
should be a nurturing environment.

Nevertheless, like Sheila, he felt uncomfortable about his position at VCRHS, regardless of how grounded in research and solid
practice he knew his work with students to be. Part of it had to do
with his knowledge that his students would not have his kind of
science classroom again at the school. The rest of the department was
committed to content acquisition. The other part was, as Sheila felt,
the terrible loneliness of being, or feeling, so different from everyone
else.

From her contact with Jacob, Sheila was learning not only the
kinds of things about group process work that she had hoped to learn
from her more immediate peers in the English department, but also

about herself from involvement in another person's struggle. Like Jacob, Sheila was outraged that some teachers were still, in effect, tracking their students in spite of the school's policy of equity. Perhaps from the perspective that his reactions offered her, however, she began to realize that it might not be useful to let oneself be so drawn into how other people in the building teach or do not teach. On March 22, 1990, she said to me: "Really, in the end, all you can do is what *you* do and hope that what *you* do will make kids like whatever it is that they're doing."

Humility

The first person Sheila collaborated with was from outside the building. Rob, a filmmaker, had been hired as artist-in-residence for part of the spring semester in 1989 to have students create a documentary video in which they interviewed Vietnam veterans and resisters. Although Rob's direct collaboration was with a social studies teacher, there were two connections that caused Sheila to become interested in the project: (a) Most of the students who worked on the video from their social studies classes were also in her English classes; and (b) from her first encounter with Rob in the faculty lounge, she found that they shared ways of thinking about both the process and the content with which he was dealing. She became involved to such an extent that Rob included her name in the Vietnam video's final credits, and thereafter used her suggestions in his post-residency presentations and in later residencies.

Sheila's recommendations to Rob were essentially a sharing of the ways in which she herself worked on projects with students. She suggested that he have students (a) keep journals and do freewriting after seeing films or interviewing their subjects and (b) get into small groups to brainstorm lists of interview questions and later to share what they had learned. For the artist, these were transformative ways of operating with students in a school. Perhaps his willingness to risk doing it her way had to do with the fact that his conception matched hers—a community effort, involving talking and listening. It helped that the product for which he was accountable was in a nontraditional form.

Watching another adult work with students in ways that she was working with some of those same students was perhaps the first direct affirmation of Sheila's teaching in that building. The collaboration with Rob may have given her the idea that team-teaching would work; thus, the attempted collaboration later that year with Ralph.

Although Sheila's early and persistent feelings about her colleagues were characterized by defensiveness against their perceived criticism of her, in that spring of 1989 she began to give some of them the benefit of the doubt. She responded as they opened up to her about their own struggle to do the cooperative learning work the department had decided to do. Because his classroom was always accessible to anyone who walked into the English office (to which it was attached), she could recognize that Ralph was indeed engaged in the kinds of experimentation that the change required, learning as he went.

She deeply respected that a person of his experience, stature, and history of success within the traditional mode would be willing to try the uncomfortable new ways. Even in the midst of their conflict during the fall 1989 semester, she could say, "I was thinking, he had it made, so it must be really hard" (October 18, 1989). From occasional informal observations as well as from their conversations, she could see that Ralph and Sally, in particular, were trying as she was to do less and less of the talking in their classrooms. She appreciated Ralph's efforts to encourage the other teachers in the department to move away from the center. He obviously took the project seriously. But that fall during the period of her extreme vulnerability, she was only beginning to distinguish whom she could trust as colleagues from who might further damage her professional self-esteem. Jane was one person who increasingly became a colleague. When Sheila noticed the work Jane was doing for students in the writing lab, she was impressed. She also saw that other people working in nontraditional ways were generally undervalued in a traditional system:

> Ernest thinks Jane is fantastic, but what I notice about our English department is that we don't value Jane. Jane gets kids to do things that no one else can get them to do.
>
> And she's an important resource. She pretty much knows how each kid learns. She takes time to find that out, and she took time to explain to me . . . and when she told me that, I realized that I can work with his process. It's not that difficult and he'll do fine in my class.

> She would be a great resource for everybody to consult
> with, if they'd listen to her. (November 10, 1989)

The relationship that Sheila was beginning to establish with
Jane—seeing what specific help Jane could in fact give and asking
directly for it—seemed to be a new direction for Sheila. Knowing
Jane's work, she had hoped initially that Jane would speak up pub-
licly for her and with her in department meetings. She had hoped
that Jane would share her own struggles rather than seeming to be
so self-assured. Sheila was learning to accept that speaking up in
public was not Jane's way.

Seeing Jane as a resource occurred just after Sheila had finally
made a phone call to Chris, who had resigned just before the fall
semester but whose teaching Sheila now knew to have been entirely
student centered. Why she had not sought out Chris's help during
the whole year when they were both in the same department is a
puzzle, understandable only in terms of the classic isolation of teachers from one another in a school building. Quite simply, they didn't
have the same lunch periods or prep periods, and meetings were
bound by prestructured agendas.

Sheila saw the connection: just as it is in classrooms for students,
schools are not set up for teachers to talk to one another about what
they are working on or what they believe (December 18, 1989). Until
she finally called Chris, she did not even know that right within her
own department had been a person who had overcome internal pressure to "cover the material" and had begun to give classroom problems back to the students. The deeper issue in that puzzle, however,
was one of trust. Sheila had been hurt by exposing her vulnerability
openly within the school building. She was unwilling to risk it again.
Now she was creating a network of support outside the school—her
friend Sharon, her former colleague Chris, me, and her own journal.
Regarding that journal, she had made a new decision to focus on the
positive:

> I started to keep like a log at school. When I get a really good
> idea, I write it down. When something seems to go really
> well I write it down, just so I can keep track of the things that
> seem to work really well for a group, just to remind myself,
> really build a repertoire that I feel comfortable with.

> There are things that I do that are successful. There *are*
> things.

Within a few weeks, by December 1, 1989, as she was beginning to
disengage from frequent conversations with Ralph, she seemed to be
having more frequent helpful conversations with Jane. On the issue
of the students' calling her class "easy":

> I think Jane has been really helpful in having me understand
> what that means from a kid. She's really interesting because
> she said, "That's like the best thing a kid could say to you. If
> the kid feels the class is easy, then it's set up so that that kid
> can learn."

By the end of January 1990, Sheila began to feel a shift in attitude
toward her. From many unexpected directions, she was being asked
to be a mentor herself. She reported in a phone call (January 26, 1990)
that Sally had asked her to be her peer coach in the program Ernest
was hoping to start. Jacob and his friend in another department, Jack,
a formerly vocal detractor, invited her to observe their classes and
give them feedback on how they managed discussions. She went, and
then invited them into her classes, so they could observe other ways
to do it (January 26, 1990).

In our interview that same day, she talked about her ideas for
Jack's class, realizing that she could be implicated in some aspects of
her critique of his tendency to do most of the talking. Loren, who had
been hired to take Chris's place, had come to Sheila for help with
everything—teaching the modules and courses Chris had designed,
setting up and managing cooperative groups and projects, and even
grading. And although she perceived it otherwise, Ralph had seen
his conversations with Sheila as ways for him to figure out how to
move through the difficulties he was having in his own classroom
(January 26, 1990).

In February 1990, Ernest, the principal of VCRHS, visited her
class. Sheila reported to me that he had seen her "most difficult class,"
but his report of it when I interviewed him the next day indicated
that what he appreciated about her was what she valued most in
herself:

> **Ernest** Sheila is an excellent teacher. I just get a kick out of sitting there and watching her interact with her students. She just seems so natural. It's obvious that she likes what she's doing. She likes the kids and they like her. Just a lot of good things going on. I've never seen her in a situation in class or outside of class working with kids that I just wasn't pleased that she was with us.
>
> **Liz** (regarding SATs) Do you have the sense that with the kind of work that Sheila is doing, because it's not the traditional stand-up-and-lecture—all of that—that the kids will be ready?
>
> **Ernest** I don't have any fear about their not being ready. . . . I have faith in . . . the methods that she utilizes . . . but as far as what it means to the kid later on, I think what she's doing is much more valuable. . . . She's able to engage all of her kids. She does a masterful job of it, I think. [From parents and the school committee], I just hear good things, and I know I hear from her colleagues in the building and her department head and other people that they are very pleased. Very pleased. (February 12, 1990)

His perception of his school, in fact, was that she was perfectly normal within it:

> We're a nontraditional school in the sense of not teaching to tests. Since we're not a tracked school any longer, there's been quite a change in approaches, a broader utilization of a variety of teaching models.
>
> And I think that one of the things that we emphasize are the thinking skills, relying on students to work out for themselves right answers.
>
> There is no one right answer and that frustrates a lot of kids who are looking for the teacher to give them the right answer, especially when you're dealing with interpretation of literature.

Sheila could have benefited from hearing Ernest say all this, directly to her, long before February 1990 when he said it to me. By the time he said it, however, she had already moved toward claiming her

own strengths and was surprised, even a little in awe, about the shift
in attitude toward her on the part of many faculty. On March 5, 1990,
she said:

> I just want to say that it could be different next week, but I
> have noticed a change. . . . At the last meeting I was very
> outspoken as usual and people came to me later to tell me
> how great it was, what I said, and that I kept saying it.

The shift seemed to be schoolwide, as Sheila reported it:

> Jane said something interesting to me Friday night. She said,
> "If you didn't do it last year, this year you've sealed your
> reputation. Kids want to take courses just 'cause you're
> teaching them. It doesn't matter what it is."
>
> Something happened. Something is starting to happen,
> and Ralph's being really great. I don't know what it is but it
> seems like the click in time is coming, so even though these
> kids are freaked out that we're reading this *Hundredth Mon-*
> *key* [Keyes, 1982] book and they think it's absurd that you
> would think about disarming, they're still doing the reading.
>
> They're doing the work, and they're doing the best work
> I've ever seen them do.

Part of a Community

Sheila thought the shift might have to do with the Women's History Month display she had created in the main lobby of the school.
At one Friday evening basketball game, she took snapshots of students' mothers, and featured these pictures as heroes in the display.
She was at the basketball game as usual, connecting her teaching to
the rich context of community. She coordinated a successful teacher-
parent dance. She organized the Celebration of Education fair. Within
the faculty, she began to take action when she felt an intervention
needed to happen for a child; she did not just wish others would take
action. By that time, she had begun to include her own needs in her
decisions about how to run things, consciously deciding to be less
confrontational, and to avoid the faculty lounge at times when she
found herself feeling more vulnerable. She talked 2 weeks later about
finding the balance between accessibility and distance with her

students. It was in that interview that she said: "There reaches a point where a teacher who has been supported gains confidence. I don't need the confirmation from people in the building" (March 5, 1990).

Now that she felt she didn't need their approval, she could affirm other teachers, especially those who were sensitive to troubled students and especially gentle men—the art teacher and Jacob. She could see allies in those men; in Sue in the math department; Barb, the guidance counselor; the librarians; and the English department, predominantly women: "Our department is just softer. We're softer with one another." What she had decided was that she wanted to remain "humble" with her colleagues. By "humble" she meant this:

> There are things I do well. There are things even people I don't like do well, and I don't think it serves purposes to vie for being the best or knowing all the answers or having it all together.
>
> It just doesn't serve any purpose but to alienate people and make them angry, because I think teachers feel bad enough about themselves to start off with. I really do.
>
> I don't think it's a profession where people feel good or smart or better. . . . I think generally speaking, people struggle between low self-esteem and needing to be the greatest. (April 27, 1990)

Once Sheila had decided to appreciate what her colleagues would do for her, it seemed that they began to do more. Perhaps Sheila had redefined "support" in broader terms. In a phone conversation a month later, Sheila told me she saw Jane as "a godsend," because Jane let her send students down to the writing lab all the time; in there "there's a real writing atmosphere." By then, the kind of affirmation that she recognized as more direct affirmation began to come to her. Referring to Sheila and Jane in terms of the fear of budget cuts, Ralph said to me:

> I can't afford to lose Sheila, because she's new and she's an innovator and I only have two people in my department that are innovators. If I lose them, then I don't have anybody to help me go through change and progress as a department. So it's important that I keep her. (May 24, 1990)

Sheila felt it coming: "I think that Ralph really knows how valuable I am to him, and that he respects me" (June 10, 1990).

> If it's true that what you put out comes back to you, I'm reaping the benefits now, because—I'm just getting a lot back and in some ways it's like justice to me. . . . What I think is that people see that I'm good: kids work for me and kids like me. They do good things, so why not recognize that? (May 24, 1990)

After the education fair that Sheila organized, both Ernest and the superintendent of schools wrote her personal letters. A parent on the parents' committee offered to write a letter saying how important she was to the school. The elementary school principal saw her on TV and wrote a letter thanking her for things she had said about how significant the work of teaching is, and for her urging that teaching needs to be honored by communities. Students were writing her letters. The seniors invited her to speak for their senior chapel. From all this honoring of her work Sheila took the message, "I realize that I am doing my job here."

She was hearing extremely supportive words from the school committee, about herself and the other teacher who might have to be cut if the budget did not pass. She told me on the phone: "One stood up in town meeting and said something about each of us, to make us real to the town. I wrote him a note: 'In my professional life I've not *been* real to anyone but my students' " (May 24, 1990).

When her car broke down and she needed to ask for rides, she realized that she did not resist allowing herself to rely on other people. She asked herself why it had been so hard for her—or for any of us—to ask one another for help (June 4, 1990). She had decided to be healthy and to achieve a clearer balance in her life, starting by trying to see the positive in things as well as seeking feedback from people she had learned she could trust.

Note

1. Especially David Johnson and Roger Johnson's (1975) *Learning Together and Alone* and Nancy Schniedewind and Ellen Davidson's (1987) *Cooperative Learning, Cooperative Lives,* which she discovered and I have since used in my own classes.

6 Developing the Mentoring Relationship

*If you work in isolation and you feel like you're an outcast, it helps
someplace to be told you're doing OK.*
                            —Sheila (Interview, December 18, 1989)

Perspective

Sheila's hiring interview had led her to expect full ongoing colleague and administrative support as she designed new ways of
working with her classes. When she realized that no one in the school
seemed prepared to offer the positive feedback and extension of her
own thinking that she had anticipated, she felt abandoned. Not until
well after Sheila was fully involved in teaching at VCRHS did she
begin to understand that she had been hired for a wider responsibility than her own classes: She was to be in the vanguard of pedagogical innovations that would fully implement the heterogeneous
grouping to which the school had committed itself.

In retrospect, as the events over the ensuing 2 years suggest, in
spite of what she felt she lacked, she may have been the person in the

school who had had the most practice in alternative pedagogies. In her prior 7 years of teaching experience, although she had effectively relied on the force of her own dynamic personality in teaching, she had begun to see the possibilities of students' creativity when she trusted them with more and more of their own decisions. In the new position at VCRHS, she felt a mandate to continue her search for concrete ways to move herself away from center stage, and to focus on allowing the students to construct much of their own knowledge. Because Sheila was struggling daily to figure out strategies and relationships within the classroom, she felt isolated, frightened, and even set up by having to be a model for veteran teachers who all seemed to her to be totally confident in what they were already doing.

According to Sheila, the shift from abandonment to connection described in Chapter 5 would not have happened without the support of an adviser who understood and shared her vision of teaching, and could extend her sense of what was possible within it. That support was crucial to her sense of herself as a teacher. In one of the earliest postobservation conferences (November 22, 1988) only a little over 3 months into the school year and our collaboration, Sheila said to me, "If it weren't for you, I'd quit teaching." At the end of the 2-year study (June 10, 1990), she named what I had helped her achieve: "perspective." That is, looking beyond the narrow confines of her classroom, her department, and her school allowed her to see all of those more clearly. From that broader perspective, she was able to focus on thinking about what she was doing rather than on what others in the school thought about it.

Although her colleagues wanted the best for their students as much as she did for hers, they routinely ignored, scoffed at, indulged, or seemed embarrassed by her enthusiasm for student-generated insights. From what she could tell, her colleagues' methods, even for small groups, was to structure lessons that carefully defined the terms in which students should think about a text, lest they miss something. Which pedagogy was more protective and more limiting of student empowerment?

The reflection that the mentoring provided allowed Sheila to recognize that she, like her colleagues, was still reluctant to allow students to struggle without her intervention at every step—part of her own insufficiently examined traditional assumptions about what students can do and about the role of a teacher. Taking the risk of letting go of a certain amount of control over what and how students read and wrote was delayed by her feeling that she was not doing her job if she did not provide them with complete guidelines that would inevitably direct them to right answers.

This was confusing for her. On the one hand, she felt guilty about not "helping" students through sometimes difficult content. On the other hand, she was being accused of "mothering" the students. After much agonizing, Sheila realized that "helping" students can take many forms. The traditional way would be to do the work—or at least the thinking—for them, so they would have all the "facts" in their notes and they would be "prepared." Trying not to do students' thinking for them traditionally meant abandoning students after assigning them to produce an independent product. Sheila figured out that it was possible to operate from neither side of that dualism.

Within the first year of our working together, she decided that a teacher's holding onto control of the meaning of a text was the more protective, and therefore more disabling, approach to teaching English. Before she could ask other faculty to understand or share her vision, however, she had to trust completely that a teacher's belief in his or her students' capacities for interdependence and self-direction would result in students' taking much of the responsibility for their own and each others' learning, as long as she designed and carefully monitored activities that were both clear enough and open enough to give them opportunity to do that. Whereas other faculty may have defined her "mothering," "nice," "easy" behaviors as creating learned helplessness, Sheila saw herself nurturing to empower, as she began clearly seeing her colleagues' reliance on worksheets, end-of-chapter questions, conventional frameworks, and even *Cliff Notes*, rather than on their own or the students' original thinking.

It took many months of self-doubt and reflection before Sheila could accept that what students referred to as "easy" meant that in her class students felt safe to learn. By the end, she boldly claimed that her nurturing of students was appropriate for a high school. It meant caring about them enough not to set them up for failure, and not to abandon them to a competitive environment. It was to be there with them, frequently checking in, until they felt able to struggle with the work of creating their own knowledge. It meant creating an environment that encouraged success without "protecting" them from creative struggle.

Letting Go of Fear of Judgment

The relationship of connectedness that Sheila had created with her students was the kind of relationship she had needed Ernest and Ralph to establish with her in her induction year at VCRHS. She needed them to trust that she could do it, not defining the work of helping as doing it for her but being consistently available to give support with interested, knowledgeable, honest, but essentially non-judgmental feedback. To have expected that kind of support in an ongoing way from a high school principal and department chair, however (especially without requesting it specifically), may have been to expect too much.

Even after she took the risk of allowing me to watch her teach 2½ months after we had begun to talk, it took her several more months to believe that I would not be evaluating her performance—that I would not be judging her as a teacher. In early September 1988 when I proposed the observations and offered the classroom-based feedback to supplement our informal conversations, she was unwilling to let me into her classroom. She recalled many months later (July 1, 1989) how she had felt the previous September:

> **Sheila** I look to you [and my friend Sharon] as people who—I have this thing where I should be like you now, but I think, these are two women who've been teaching for years, many more years than I have, know more things than I do. I have to tell myself that it's OK that we're not all the same. I think mentor people can be very intimidating. . . . People that I know are good at what they do, who know a lot, those people I find a little bit intimidating.
>
> **Liz** How did you get over it?
>
> **Sheila** Well, I know that I really want to be a better teacher, and I really want to have help, and . . . I realize that you can help me and that you weren't going to say I was bad or wrong. You were just going to help me, and you were also very positive. You said a lot of really good things that I thought to myself, oh, there's some good things, too.

My admiration for her teaching made it easy for me not to judge her; she was doing what I had always hoped to see in action. Above all, I admired her struggle. Her fear of my judgment appeared to diminish as visit after visit I offered feedback that affirmed what she was trying to do. When she requested my input, I asked questions and offered specific suggestions from my own experience and from research that might help her manage assignments and tasks. I also offered metaphors that might help her reconceive her role: I recommended that she "jigsaw" (Aronson, 1978) when the amount of material she wanted to have students "cover" seemed overwhelming; that she think of furniture and students in space the way a choreographer might; and that she visualize her own relationship to small interdependent groups as if she were a waitress, unobtrusive but alert and available, freeing herself from them but fully involved from a distance.

Problem-Solving Dialogue

I made most of my active suggestions in parts in the first year of visits with her (November 1988 through May 1989), with some occurring in conversations during April vacation and in the summer of that year. Thereafter, my active interventions seemed to be concentrated in the difficult fall semester of 1989. During those interventions, I asked questions about how she had made particular decisions. Active listening and dialogue gave her plenty of time to reflect aloud in my presence. The transcripts of those dialogues are predominantly Sheila's words: perhaps 80%. Otherwise, my comments focused on the positive things I saw actually happening in her classrooms, reminding her of the power of her original vision.

The effect of the nonjudgmental dialoguing appeared to be that Sheila no longer showed signs of feeling intimidated by me. In later interviews, she directly confirmed that change. From almost the beginning but certainly by the spring of 1989, Sheila was introducing me to her classes as a person who was going to help her become a better teacher. Ultimately, we could not miss seeing the connection between the safe space Sheila created within her classroom for her students to grow and the safety and trust that grew for her within our research relationship.

It was clear that that trust was already in operation when I visited on January 17, 1989: "I have a lot of anxiety about this activity I've planned for using groups, but I'm going to do it anyway because you're here."

She sometimes restructured her activities for later classes in terms of my comments from earlier ones in the same day: about her own voice level when students were in groups, how desks might be arranged, or what kind of guidelines might turn an assignment into one in which the students could generate for themselves and with one another the meanings in a piece of literature. She risked trying out things she had never thought of trying before, processing with me minute details about how they might go and afterward how they had gone and what she could do next.

Discovering and Dealing With the Pivotal Anxiety: Content

The early April 1989 dialogue is the only one in which my own comments approach 30% to 40% of the conversation. My function in this interview seemed to be to recall her to her vision and to help counter her insecurity about how to let students find in a text what there was to find. She did not yet trust the group process or her own skill in setting up activities that would get them into the work. How to get them to engage? She assigned me an observation task:

> **Sheila** Look at what the groups do, because I don't believe they
> can do it. . . . I *do* believe, but I'm afraid that they're going to
> miss stuff.
> **Liz** So what if they miss stuff?
> **Sheila** I don't know. I feel like then I don't do my job.

That anxiety felt like a key one to me. I had heard it as well from many preservice and in-service teachers, and continue to hear it well after this study. Within the process of our conversation that day, it occurred to me that although Sheila had been working to move away from the center of her teaching, her focus was still content centered. She still assumed a body of knowledge that she required herself to cover. I asked her if she wanted to take the leap from content-centered teaching to student-centered teaching:

> **Sheila** I've always admitted to being—I'm a guider. I do that,
> which doesn't allow them necessarily to have their own

thoughts. I *am* very content centered, I agree—content as I have decided it goes.

Liz So maybe that last leap is to let go of whether they get everything that's gettable in the literary work or in the textbook, and seeing what, as kids—9th grade, 10th grade, whatever they are—they *can* get.

Sheila OK, and then what do you do with what they get?

Liz (Laughs) What *do* you do with what they get?

Sheila (Pause) I don't know. I don't know all the time.

Liz (Pause) I think we've found the bottom line for you, Sheila.

Sheila Yeah.

Liz The feeling that "they won't get it unless I tell them."

Sheila Yeah.

Liz And you're not standing up there lecturing and telling them, but you're telling them in the questions.

Sheila Yeah, I'm pretty much gearing how they work together. Yeah, I know.

Liz And gearing how they look at the very work.

Sheila Yeah, I am. . . . Maybe I think that's what I'm supposed to be doing. I think that's it. Plus . . . I'm not really sure how to arrange an activity so that they're doing something. I'm not convinced that they'll *do* anything. So maybe I have to *see* that they'll really be able to talk to one another.

Liz So can we play with that and see?

Sheila (Pause, then with a changed voice) OK, let's do this. There are, actually there are six poems . . .

She was ready to try to trust the students with only the text and one another, without her intervention: six groups and six Whitman poems and the question, "What does the poet feel, and how do you know?"

Her agreeing to risk that total change in her curricular agenda seems to have been the pivotal decision of her teaching during our 2-year professional relationship. The rest of that dialogue is her brainstorming, partly with me but mostly with herself, about how to set up the lesson around that assignment. As we were talking in her empty classroom, we overheard Ralph next door, seeming to be lecturing to his class in the background. In the immediacy of this brief dialogue, Sheila realized that she had been mistaking appearances for a much more complicated reality:

Sheila See, he tells them everything they're supposed to know. But he doesn't think that he does. But maybe he isn't.

Liz But you were thinking you weren't doing that, because they were sitting in groups.

Sheila Because they were sitting in groups.

Once she could see her own deep-seated distrust of letting go of control over the content, she was able to talk about seeing what other habits or attitudes were getting in the way of her working toward more student-centeredness:

> I think that I take over, so I'm worried that it won't work 'cause I take over, and probably that's always what happens. I'm a boss. I'm a big boss. I am, I know, and I have trouble letting them struggle. I feel like they're not going to do anything. That's anxiety making for me.
>
> I mean I know in my brain that's the way to do it, but I'm reluctant to do it that way, 'cause I don't know what they'll come up with and then I don't necessarily know what to do with what they've come up with.
>
> I'm confused . . . if I have to answer to people about the kids knowing certain stuff, I'm worried about that, and I feel like I'm held accountable. . . . Trying to decide what they do need to know is scary. (April, 1990)

The important thing was that she was willing to try. She said that willingness came from her having right there with her while she tried it a person who could offer immediate feedback, constant reassurance from the research, and the structured opportunity to hear herself talk it all through.

After the first try that day, I described the good things I had seen happening in the class: (a) her care to have the students move the desks into discrete groups, (b) her having validated what students said, (c) the students making interesting points, and (d) the students sometimes even listening to one another.

Those descriptions of what she had experienced in spite of her anxieties allowed her to believe with a part of herself:

> **Sheila** So you think if they practice this enough I'll get better and they'll get better?

Liz I do.

Sheila I do think what they were doing was good. I thought some of the things they were thinking of were good.

Liz They were excellent.

Sheila But I do feel—that's not true. I was going to say that I feel I could have had the same responses in a larger group with me controlling it (laughs). It probably is not true. I think what I know that's true is that if they get in the habit of making their own meaning, that's the skill. Like if someone asks me, "What's the skill that you want kids to know?" I would want them to be able to read something and figure it out. So that's it.

Focusing on the Positive

That April 1989 dialogue was the one in which she most directly asked for help with a process that felt new to her. Frequently she asked me, "You think . . .?"; "Is it OK to . . .?"; "Could they?"; "Can I . . .?"; she also asked of herself and me, "What if . . .?" She and I worked through the "what ifs" together, with "OK, let's figure that out." Halfway through our brainstorming together, she worried: "Wait 'til you see what happens!" Then she caught herself not trusting: "I'm not going to say that. That's not fair." I answered, "So let's see what happens." When she felt ready with the whole lesson, she summarized it for herself and for me, ending with, "OK?" I laughed at that checking with me. So did she:

> **Sheila** Good thing it's the last period of the day.
>
> **Liz** Are you scared?
>
> **Sheila** Uh, I have anxiety about it. Yeah!
>
> **Liz** What do you think? What's the anxiety?
>
> **Sheila** I think it's worth trying. I don't know what we're going to be able to do. (Pause) So we'll find out.

Apart from specific suggestions followed by specific feedback, Sheila seemed to be wanting reassurance that I believed completely that students can struggle for meaning and find it for themselves. In that dialogue, as in many others, I gave her that reassurance.

She was later able to name a hindrance to trusting this way of working, a way of thinking that she recognized in herself and identified as something most other teachers also are blocked by—the tendency to focus on the negative aspects of a class while overlooking the positive. My role of describing those positive aspects and recalling them to her attention turned out to be one of the most important functions I served for Sheila. On May 9, 1989, part of the conversation after a class went like this:

Sheila What I heard them doing was really good. . . . See, I chose who they worked with. Maybe I shouldn't have done that.

Liz Both of them learned something from having been with a partner who was active.

Sheila See, the bad part is that these two aren't real movers either, so that was hard.

Liz But they did move, and they did come up with some interesting stuff.

Sheila I feel very comfortable letting them choose the pairs. I didn't today.

Liz And of course they said, "You never let us choose the pairs." You handled that very nicely.

Sheila Oh, I don't even remember that.

Liz You can be really proud that they did so much with it ["The Lady or the Tiger" (Stockton, 1893)].

Sheila Well, it was kind of a battle. I didn't know what to do. I thought maybe we should read the story together. You know, all through my mind I had all these ideas. You know, "What should we do? Should I stop them?" Then I decided, I'm just going to see what they do. I know the group and I know how they work.

Liz I bet that was hard for you.

Sheila Oh, God, I didn't know what to do! Plus I felt bad. I'm like, here *you* are, and they're not doing anything! (Both laugh.) They're doing nothing! But I'd like you to see that class again, because I like that class. I think actually they're doing some very good work, and in some ways I feel the most willing to give up my control with them, as opposed to my other groups, because I *think* that I give up control but I don't always. So with them I feel that I let them—I've tried to let them make their own meaning out of things the best, so it would be worth it maybe to see them again.

By the end of that school year (mid-June, 1989), she had gained perspective about how far she had come through her own insecurity:

> **Sheila** This probably was my best year. I think it's finally because I feel I know how to do *some* things right. . . . I think a really fine teacher is rare. I think you fall into patterns of behavior that from the beginning are not correct and you just keep doing those things over and over. But they're only working for the teacher. . . . I knew how to make the classroom work for *me*. I told kids what to do and they sit there and they do it and I walk around and it's easy. I can do that. I've done it, but it stops the kids from doing anything. It's hard when you change the rules in the classroom. It's really hard. But you have to really know what you're doing. . . . I think some things work on instinct, but I don't know, or you don't stick with it long enough.
>
> **Liz** Right. You don't trust it.
>
> **Sheila** Right. 'Cause I would try a group for like 2 weeks, and that would be enough—I couldn't take it—I had to switch back to doing it differently, because it seemed too crazy for me. I couldn't take it. I didn't think anyone was getting anywhere. And they didn't trust each other, so they wouldn't listen to what each other said. I couldn't take that. Plus, if you don't see anyone modeling it, you don't know.

Although I never actually modeled it for her, I did reflect back to her what her own initial successes at student-centeredness had been, and this seemed to be what she needed. It was the only feedback she was getting because, as she told me in a phone call (July, 1989), there was no one at VCRHS who could model for her:

> I can't really get the help I need at Valley Central. Ralph just assumes I'm good, and they all do, and that's no help. He tries to stay away from feedback, unless I ask him directly— maybe I'll do that—because he doesn't want teachers to feel they're being evaluated.
>
> But he can't help me, anyway—he's struggling, he's new at this stuff himself.

Here Sheila confirmed that most teachers, including herself, assume that to have someone observe and give feedback is to open oneself up to evaluation. Her journal from 2 weeks before that phone conversation acknowledged that allowing me to come into her class every 2 weeks that year had required her to give up her autonomy. Our relationship had exposed and magnified the issues she had around her role as teacher. It was a risky choice, letting me into her room. She wrote:

> I guess autonomy gave me the space to make mistakes, so in some ways I could bear the disappointment, but more than that, I could deal with not knowing how to change to make it better. Now, I am forced to confront what I see as my own inadequacies. This is frightening. It is also exciting.
>
> Having Liz in class makes me really vulnerable. I want her to think I am good. I am afraid that she will see all of my weaknesses.
>
> I'm not sure why I am so worried about this, but I am. I know that she won't criticize me or hurt me, but I think I'm afraid to let her down. I think that often the anonymity of the classroom allows a teacher to believe that he or she is really doing fine, never *really* knowing for sure.
>
> The knowing part is the hardest. (July 19, 1989)

That summer of 1989, I shared with Sheila some of the writing I had done, describing my own long awkward struggle toward student-centered teaching (Aaronsohn, 1988). It helped her to know that it had not been at all easy for me either, and I too was still learning how to do it better. My having already thought through some of the things she was thinking through and my taking seriously the issues she took seriously was another kind of help that she did not get at her school. For example, when she was deeply troubled that a series of ninth-grade group stories had been full of violence against women, she had gone to the guidance office and then to Ralph for advice before she discussed it with me:

Liz What did they say?
Sheila Nothing. They all—we all just sort of complained, that this was a problem. But there were no suggestions. Then I felt like no one really knew what to do. It wasn't like they

were not helpful; they just didn't know. And [until you suggested it] I never would have thought of the idea of having the kids go back and rewrite it from the woman's perspective!

Need for Support

By the time she wrote in her journal on September 18, 1989, a year into our collaboration, Sheila had decided that as risky as it was to allow me to come into her classroom, "Support is the most important component in feeling like I can be successful at teaching in new ways. Alone, I would give up, become like everyone else, simply to be accepted."

However, my support of her was not enough to help her overcome the most persistent doubts, especially during the fall of 1989 when those doubts were repeatedly reinforced. I had suggested to Sheila in a phone call (October 1, 1989) that because of similar experiences I had had, it occurred to me that perhaps what her students meant by "easy" when they referred to her class was that they felt it to be nonthreatening, a place in which they could feel competent rather than afraid. She did not come to believe that, however, until she had heard it and seen it in many different ways—from another English teacher at VCRHS, from the students, and especially from her own long-term assessment of the real rigor of what she was asking her students to do. On October 20, 1989, she already knew that isolation-based fear was blocking her vision: "I'm convinced I'd become just like everyone else if there weren't people I respect saying, 'This is what the research says is best for kids, and you have to keep trying it.' I get afraid."

Not again until our November 13, 1989, dialogue was I as directive with Sheila as I had been in April of that year. The week before that visit, she had left a message on my phone machine and reluctantly acknowledged that she was in need of what I was able to give her: "I was sort of hoping that you could call me tonight, Liz. I just need some infor—I need some *support!*"

When we spoke on the phone again the day before my scheduled visit, she told me, "My self-esteem isn't strong. I just don't feel good about myself, and I don't know what to do." I asked her, "What do you *want* to do in your class?" and she began to design the method she preferred: "I want to stop the movie and let them talk. I don't want to give them worksheets."

While talking with her at the school the next day, because of her intensified insecurities, I elaborated concrete strategies by which Sheila could find out whether the students saw that she was in fact giving them what they needed. This was the day she had been ready, in her panic for his approval, to give her students the same work-sheets that Ralph had created for his section of their course, even though the two sections were doing different book-film combinations.

I affirmed the way she had handled the viewing of *The Heart Is a Lonely Hunter* (McCullers, 1967)—rewinding to play a certain scene again and having them talk about what they saw the second time through to help clear up a disagreement among students:

> **Liz** Oh, that was wonderful! It was fantastic!
> **Sheila** I loved that! That was the best!
> **Liz** Because you were going back for evidence: "Let's look at the text." And you can do that with a film; that's what's possible with videotape. You can do that constantly: "Let's go back and see."
> **Sheila** And you think that's an OK way to do it?
> **Liz** I think that's the only way to do it. It's a model for how they should do it themselves, checking the facts.

I made specific suggestions that reinforced her choice:

> **Liz** I think I might have stopped the movie a whole lot sooner, to get some of those predictions and observations.
> **Sheila** Yeah, get them to do more predicting.

Finally, I pressed her to declare her faith in her instincts, by declaring my own:

> **Liz** Can you trust that you can see the positive things that you *are* preparing them for?
> **Sheila** You're convinced that this is OK?
> **Liz** Absolutely.
> **Sheila** Given the fact that I get better at it.

Liz Absolutely convinced. I gave you my criticisms that had to do with accuracy in hearing their responses . . .

Sheila Right.

Liz . . . and management of the class, and where you would stop the movie compared to where I would, . . .

Sheila Yeah.

Liz . . . where I'd stop the film for conversation or for them just to freewrite. But except in those terms, there is no way that what you are asking them to do is wrong for kids, and you can justify it completely to them, although they may not be able to understand it. (November 13, 1989)

Because she was feeling so shaky, I reflected back to her what I had seen her accomplish in that class that she was so anxious to have accomplished, in terms that Ralph would recognize:

Liz You didn't give them guiding questions? But you did give them guiding questions.

Sheila Yes, but I did not put them on a worksheet. And I'm not telling them, I did not tell them what to look for.

Liz But you did tell them. You asked them to "predict what the movie is going to be about." You asked them for predictions, you told them to take down what they think is important. That's a guideline. You asked them for what's important. They told you. It got generated. You did! You gave them very clear structure, absolutely clear structure. It just wasn't on a worksheet and you didn't use the terms *character, plot, setting, theme, symbol*. At the end of the semester, you can translate what you've done into the literary terms that will fit, because they *were* taught the concepts; you just didn't use those particular terms. You can teach them the other language, and then they'll be prepared. (November 13, 1989)

Then I asked Sheila what if students accused her of betraying them by not giving them what other classes were learning. She role-played her response:

Well, I guess I would tell them that what *they* think is the most important thing to me, so I need to start with what they think, and if it meant that they didn't get like somebody else's analysis, that they didn't get *my* analysis, I'd be willing to tell them we could have a meeting where I gave them my analysis.

Because they might not say it in the same way that I would say it or Ralph would say it, but they would still say it. (November 13, 1989)

The transcript of our December 1, 1989, conversation is full of Sheila's acknowledgment of her need for support. She knew that she needed to share with a like-minded person what she was experiencing, learning, and struggling with in her classroom and with whom she could share her anxieties about feeling criticized by most of her colleagues. There seemed to be no one in the school who shared her fundamental assumptions about teaching and learning apart from Jacob, with whom she had only very recently begun to talk. Even that sharing was occasional and rushed. It seemed that everything else in the environment had been telling her she was teaching all wrong and only I had been there to tell her, with specific evidence that she could not deny, that she was doing fine.

In her previous job, she had had such support from her department chair. Not having it—especially not having it from Ralph, the English department chair at VCRHS—felt like a real deprivation to her. In the December 1, 1989, conversation, after an intense dialogue about whether it was personal about her or whether it was just not Ralph's way to praise anyone as directly as she seemed to need it, she began to reach deeper for sources of support. She talked about her own high school teacher whom she had so greatly respected that she had wanted to become like her:

Sheila I wanted to *be* Margaret Smith. To me she was a good woman. She was a mother, had 10 children. Ran the school, was the headmistress, but also taught. And I thought, "She's a good woman." And all my life I wanted to *be* her. . . . She knew me as a person. I guess I want to be like her.

Liz Maybe you are. It sounds like you are.

Sheila Yeah, I'm probably a lot like her.

Liz So can you accept that you're wonderful too, like her?

Sheila Like today I almost wanted to tell myself I was wonderful because I really thought what my students were doing was good, but sometimes I'm just not sure. Like I would like for someone else to say, "This is good."

Receiving the "Mothering" She Gives

The caring feedback and the "unconditional positive regard" that Sheila knew she needed was exactly what she gave to her students. Her discovery that high schools are not generally set up to value or give time to nurturing caused her great distress. She and I discussed the situation in which she found herself and her feelings about it. We wondered together about the extent to which nurturing behavior is understood to be a gendered activity in North American culture and, therefore, the extent to which the devaluing of it amounts to a de-valuing of what women do. My own initial research on high school teachers' reluctance to use cooperative learning confirmed her obser-vations. I had found, among other factors, however benevolently rendered, characteristics commonly associated in Western culture with authoritarian fathers: judging, hierarchy, focus on product and measurable achievement rather than on process, and impatience with process and with relationship (Aaronsohn, 1988).

Her frequent reference to this aspect of high school teaching sug-gests that the most disturbing issue for Sheila of that late fall of 1989 had to do with how her identity as a woman was perceived by her colleagues. Ralph had told her more than once in ways that she in-terpreted as disapproval that she was treating her students as if she were their mother. She understood him to be saying that her nurtur-ing attitude toward students was inconsistent with the role of a high school teacher. By December 18, 1989, her confusion and isolation around this pivotal issue were diminishing as she developed a po-litical perspective on the distancing academic posture characteristic of teacher- and content-centered teaching:

I guess, I—I need to not accept those criticisms for being a woman, because that's what I am, and I think—I mean I think other women in the building either become like the men or they're penalized. And there are probably other women who feel the same way.

But I think it's not OK for us to be women. I feel that way.

Sheila claimed that she got to that point in her thinking because she had a person to give back to her the reality of what her own "mothering" of students looked like and how it could be seen from both a research perspective and a personal perspective as better for students, even high school students.

She had begun to move toward believing what I was saying about mothering because she had begun to trust our relationship:

> I need to believe that what will work *will* work, and you'll help me figure out ways to get groups to do things together. I really appreciate your support. It's really important to me.
>
> It's hard to know if it's going OK. . . . Sometimes I don't know how to measure whether it's working. I've been asking the wrong people. *You're* just coming into my classroom to listen.
>
> I want the classes to be discussion based, so kids are really talking to each other. I have to set up tasks requiring them to talk and then do something. . . . I just want you to know how important it is to have *you* tell me I'm on the right track.
>
> Talking with you reminds me that it's OK not to be like everybody else. In fact, it's probably better. But it's hard. I think if you work in isolation and you feel like you're an outcast, it helps someplace to be told you're doing OK. (December 18, 1989)

One of the best things I was able to give her that late fall was a transcript of her own words from before that difficult fall semester to remind her of her own vision. She said:

> I need to be able to say to myself, like maybe if I play the tape and just listen to my own self saying—because I started reading the document that you gave me, and I thought, "This is great!" I thought, "I said this? This is great!" (December 18, 1989)

A Mirror

Sheila felt strongly that it was my regular observation of her work and my creating a mirror for her that was helping her grow:

I know that a lot of folks are saying one thing but doing another, and I think that really scares me, that people could say they're doing something but not really do it, and maybe you don't even know you're not doing it until someone tells you.

Because if people aren't watching you, you'll never really know what you're doing. (June, 1989)

The mirror my visits provided helped her see herself and her students:

This year I really can see a marked improvement. But I let myself see it. I don't think in the past I let myself really watch that, stand back enough to watch them grow. This year I really can see it. . . . There's something neat in watching them come to that realization of what they can do. (June, 1989)

This was a clearer sense for Sheila of what she was after. She knew she had more to learn, however, and was looking forward to another try: "[This year was] a little bit better. I think it was different. I think next year will be better. I think it's going to be a lot better. I hope" (June, 1989).

The work was not only a matter of designing lessons and managing a new kind of classroom. The work, she understood as of July 1, 1989, was on her own attitudes about herself and other people:

But I get into that mind-set: "Oh, if I'm not good at everything I'm terrible, I stink, I should quit." I used to do that. "Oh, I should quit! I'm horrible!"

This was my first year where I began to realize there are some things I do well, and there are some things I need help with, and people will help me if I ask them, but they won't try to *get* me.

I like what I'm doing. We'll solve the problems, nothing is horrible, no one will be punished. There are other things, however, that I'm not good at, and I've also been programmed. To have kids write in personae is a new thing for me, to get away from feeling like you have to write a formal essay, be formal about everything. I mean I felt like I had to teach kids that.

Well, I think [the formal essay] is one thing they can learn how to do, but it's not the only thing, and I also think when they're really thinking and really engaged is when they're writing either "I think this" or "I think that" or they're a persona or they're acting something out. (June 16, 1989)

"Good" Teacher Redefined

Dialogues from the new semester, which started in January 1990 with new 10-week modules and semester courses, reveal the spiral nature of Sheila's development of confidence. They convey her relief in coming back to autonomy in her classes: She was no longer team-teaching with Ralph. They also show, however, that her sense of self had been so shaken by the challenges of the previous semester that she was still struggling to justify her own way of working as academically legitimate. She said long afterward that our support relationship made the return of self a much easier one after this setback than it had been originally during her first academic year at VCRHS.

Our dialoguing worked on her identity as a teacher. The concern she still expressed on January 7, 1990, was about what she perceived as her students' reluctance to believe that her way of teaching was as valid as the traditional way that had been ingrained in them. She claimed with dismay that her students had been programmed to recognize who was a "good" teacher: "In any school where I've worked, the teacher that sat at the desk and gave all the information was always thought of as the best teacher, because they *knew* everything. They appeared to *know* everything."

She knew that she did not fit that definition and that she did not want to. But she did want to be considered a "good" teacher. Talking it all through as I listened and acknowledged, she sorted out contradictions. She knew, on the one hand, that it was still important to her to "fit in" and have the kind of solid reputation she perceived Ralph to have. She also knew, on the other hand, that she was already respected for being who she was and for teaching the way she taught: "But I know that people like Travis's parents love me because I let their kid be himself. He felt good enough to be himself. He felt good enough to do good things."

She also knew and appreciated along with me in our conversation 3 weeks later that there were things going on in her classroom for which she had reason to be proud. By that interview

(January 26, 1990), she was already feeling much more as if what was going on was what she had hoped would go on. Her self-assurance was so clear that I said:

> You know why I love working with you? Whenever I ask you a question about why you chose to do something in your class, even a very small thing like how people are sitting together, you always have thought about it, and you always have a very very good reason for it (Sheila laughs).
>
> Really, it's true. You're not just justifying. You're saying, "I thought about that. I noticed it and I decided not to make any changes in it for this reason."

Her response acknowledged growing competence in this pedagogy focused on the students and their needs:

> I think if someone asks me what is one of the most important teaching skills, I'd say assessment. Like I have to really quickly assess—"OK, what's the deal here? What should I do? How far should I go?"—and decide very quickly.
>
> I could have said, "OK, I want you to sit this way," but it's not the right time for that now, and it could do some damage. . . . I was aware of what was happening.

Her self-confidence was not yet there enough to keep her from being surprised when I acknowledged what I saw to be a shift in our relationship:

> **Liz** I want to tell you that there's no way that I would ask you to change anything, because I think I'm at the stage now with this stuff that I'm learning more from you . . .
> **Sheila** (Gasps)
> **Liz** . . . than you're learning from me.
> **Sheila** You're kidding! Really?
> **Liz** Um.
> **Sheila** I'm really surprised about that.
> **Liz** Why?
> **Sheila** Well, just because most of the things that I do now I didn't do 3 years ago. (February 12, 1990)

Without denying the compliment, she talked a great deal through that interview about how hard the transformation still was. This time, however, her reaction to its being "hard" was a hopeful, confident one: "We all have to practice." Nevertheless, by the end of that interview, she was still feeling isolated at VCRHS in spite of her pleasure with how things were going within her classroom. She said she was considering going back to graduate school: "If I was back at graduate school I would be getting some other feedback. That would be really good because I really don't get any around here, and I've been noticing that that could be hard."

Mentoring

No Investment

By the time of our March 20, 1990, conversation, Sheila had completely given up wishing that she could get feedback "around here." As she would say, "something clicked in" between March 5 and March 20. On March 5 when she said, "I think that you need somebody to check in with that says, 'You're all right. The way you're doing it is all right,' " she was still hoping to hear it from the VCRHS faculty or students:

> I never hear someone say, "You know, it's all right." It would
> be really great if someone would say, "You know, Miss M.,
> you're really kooky, but it's all right" (laughs).

She had almost given up that expectation, however, because she was getting and allowing herself to accept as such, good support from her close friends, Sharon and Ron, who were teachers in another state:

> When I get a little scared about the way that I do things, when
> I talk with them I feel recommitted, because I know other
> people: they are people who do the things that I do, even
> more so—even more so. (March 5, 1990)

Now, instead of longing for what people could not give her, Sheila had come to the conclusion that it had probably been useful, however hard, that the feedback she had gotten had been from some-one outside the school who "has no investment":

> So I definitely think something has changed. I think probably part of it is just getting comfortable, me growing up, but I think that that happens by talking: I don't think it just hap-pens by being introspective yourself.
>
> I think you need to have someone to give you the feed-back that has no investment, that has no need to say, "Well, I need you to be better." That has no investment. That can completely just say, "OK, this is what I saw," free from any association. I think that's critical.
>
> And I just maybe think, looking enough at it—I mean I think that's what you provide, is a sort of a mirror, to look at it: "This is what was happening and this is what happened, this is what didn't happen, this seemed to be working, and how about this?" I think because of that I've been willing to take more risks. (March 20, 1990)

The Risk of Openness

When Sheila first allowed me to interview a broad selection of her students in the spring of 1989, she was as eager as I was to dis-cover their perceptions of the kind of work she was doing with them. The feedback I gave her after I had listened to the first three groups of three and four students made her feel that most of them were pleased with her methods. Furthermore, she thought that the intense listening to, interest in, and respect for their views of which the in-terview process consisted was a thing that should go on more often between adults and students, if only there were time.

It helped Sheila that I was able to summarize for her the gist of the interviews I had conducted with some of her students again at the end of that fall semester. They were all aware that in the class she was team-teaching with Ralph, she was teaching like him and not like herself. One student who also had a different class with her said,

Student But when she's on her own, like in our class, it's dif-ferent.
Liz So she's freer with you?
Student Right.

In the spring of 1990, some seniors said they were feeling betrayed, as she had predicted, though not for the reasons she had assumed while she was managing her way through that difficult period. She had thought they would be angry at her for not preparing them for expectations in more traditional classrooms to come, but their disappointment was actually over her change of personality, style, and expectations of them during the fall of 1989. They told me on March 5, 1990, what they felt: By becoming less authentic in her behavior, and especially by asking them to meet standards she did not really believe in, she had compromised their relationship with her.

Despite some students' defense of her academic intentions and despite her understanding of all the reasons why others might have had leftover reasons to be angry at her, Sheila felt vulnerable and even attacked when I summarized for her the feelings I had heard in the small groups. Her anger at my having served as a catalyst for their expression of discontent shook our relationship. Her response made me feel that I had been insensitive, had intruded, had violated professional conduct, and had overstepped my bounds. I had lost her trust. It was a very difficult few hours, during which I had to call into question and reconstruct the boundaries of my overlapping roles of researcher, mentor, friend, and advocate of student-centered teaching.

It was as if her initial fears about allowing me in had been confirmed. No one else in the building, she said, had put themselves in a position of being so harshly and arbitrarily criticized by their students in the presence of an adult who listened so carefully and took them so seriously. Although the careful, serious attention to students' voices was what she advocated and had appreciated in the former interviews, she felt this one had gone too far.

If this had happened earlier or within a more fragile relationship between us, especially one in which the power dynamic had been more unequal, that incident might have aborted the study, if not the friendship. Within the solid previous experience of trust and mutual growth through reflection, however, Sheila sorted through her feelings and declared herself ready to continue.

Before that incident and again once we had worked it through both separately and together, my position of being there "with no investment" and especially with no power meant that she was free to sort through her feelings about her students' reactions without having to worry about how I was hearing them or her. She could use me, even in a situation in which I had been a catalyst for knowledge that made her very uncomfortable, as a person with whom to figure out what to do about what she was learning.

Courage

Sheila understood from the outset that she was taking a risk in allowing me access to her classroom, to her thoughts, and, as described above, without her intervention, to her students. She could have discontinued our relationship at any time if my presence had continued to distress her. She had started out feeling insecure about exposing her teaching to my scrutiny. By the end of that academic year, she realized that her own fear of exposure was probably a common one for teachers:

> We want to say, "I do process writing, I do cooperative learning," but we aren't really doing it. But we want to say that we are, because that's what we're supposed to be doing, but we don't know how.
>
> And we're afraid, but we don't want to say, "I don't know how." I think this year what I learned to say is, "I don't know how to do that. Will you show me?"
>
> There's that fear of thinking, "Ask for help? I shouldn't be. I'm a professional! Ask for help? What does that say? I'll be uncovered that I don't know what I'm doing." (June 12, 1990)

It took courage to allow me in despite that fear. It took the same kind of courage to accept my suggestions for more student-centered processes in the face of her persistent feeling, expressed strongly in the two April interviews, that she would be seen as not doing her job if she operated a classroom "my way," as much as that appealed to her own vision of how students learn best: "I'm confused. I have to answer to people about the kids knowing certain stuff, I'm worried about that and I feel like I'm held accountable" (July 1, 1989).

She understood from her previous teaching jobs, as well as from the way things were done at VCRHS, that what she valued about students' productivity was not what was generally valued by other teachers or by parents. So she was afraid. She did it anyway. In very early September 1989, she reported, "It's kind of scary when you're trying new things. I bit off all my fingernails, and I have diarrhea."

As she began to do the actual work, she put her anxious energy into creating lessons. The decisions she was asking the students to make within all her classes involved them as well as her in significant risk taking. For example, what if they chose their own groups?

> I think what will happen this time is that, let's say five people pick their friends, and they're not working very well. That gives us an opportunity to look at the process, like to say, "How's it going? Why isn't it working? Maybe it's not working because you're all buddies? Is that a problem? And if it's a problem, what are you going to do to solve it? Because this is your group."
>
> So it might be a really good opportunity to have them work with that process. It could be a complete bomb, but that's a risk they took when they decided they wanted to choose. I think that's fair. (September 18, 1989)

Her willingness to let a content lesson "bomb" in order for the students to practice making effective choices seemed to have developed as a direct result of her April-May 1989 recognition that her focus on the importance of content contradicted her faith in students. But what a risky use of time! She was not over the anxiety by September of 1989, even though she was working through it: "In the beginning I was really worried about it, but now I see that it's moving along." She was coming to terms with her fear of getting in trouble for getting rid of a textbook in favor of letting students choose their own readings:

> In some ways it was scary because you think, "Well, what if a kid reads all S. E. Hinton?" Well, what if they do?
>
> I just read a great article in *English Journal* where it said, "If kids like it, it can't be literature." Well, why not? If you want them to read, why are you giving them things that they hate?

That sounded pretty confident, but she was still in conflict about her role:

> **Sheila** It's really hard to let them struggle.
>
> **Liz** Why is it hard to have them struggle?
>
> **Sheila** Well, I just feel like—I feel like it's my job to help them. So if they're struggling, I'm not helping them, and I'm not supposed to *do* that. I'm supposed to be the helper person.

She spoke of her fundamental fear: "If you say 'anything is possible,' what if you can't control what they come up with? It's kind of scary" (September 18, 1989). She recognized this fear in herself but felt preceded in walking through fear. She told me that people she admired were like giraffes—they stuck their necks out. She could do it too.

It was not easy for her. She told me on the phone (November, 1989): "I'm still nervous about your being there when I'm not sure what I'm doing." That was a year after we had begun. She let me come anyway. When we talked in specifics the next day about a class I had just observed, she was open to a suggestion: "We could try that. I mean that's a possibility." Nevertheless, despite the wonderful work she was seeing the students in her classes do, she was still concerned about her own accountability:

> **Liz** You didn't trust it. You were afraid.
>
> **Sheila** I'm still scared. The whole thing makes me really nervous because I think, see, the kids will talk to each other and the kids in [Ralph's] class will say, "We're doing this," and the kids in my class will say, "We're not doing that. Miss M., the goof ball, she's not doing anything."

But she did it anyway.

"Whatever It Is Will Be OK"

The March 22, 1990, interview was the one in which Sheila most explicitly connected my mentoring to her changed feelings about her teaching. She had moved from being intimidated by me and from reluctance to allow me to watch her teach, through fear that she would let me down and through the vulnerability my presence caused, to eagerness for what she would learn from our conversations. In the difficult fall of 1989, my role was to continue to believe in her when she could not believe in herself. In the period of transition from that hard time, I was her colleague, her friend, and her listener—

always her listener. Now I was someone with whom to share whatever happened:

> I guess in some ways it's confidence, because I guess *I* have
> decided that *my* agenda is legitimate. The things that are
> important to me are legitimate. And I think *that* comes from
> the feedback.
>
> Like now I think, OK, you'll come up Thursday, and
> you'll see things, and you'll tell me what you see and what
> you think. But I already—I'm not afraid of it, at all. I already
> know that it will be OK.
>
> I'm not worried that nothing will happen, because I
> know that something will, and whatever it is will be OK.

In that conversation Sheila noted the parallels between the way we
were working together and the way she worked with her students:
listening, validating, questioning, giving feedback, encouraging, and
telling them when they were "great." She said:

> Well, I think that's exactly what you do when you teach writ-
> ing, right? . . . "If that's what you want to say, OK! Just talk!"
> And I think for me—I mean, I don't know if this is true for
> other people, but I think it's hearing myself talk things
> through that makes it more clear, but doing it over and over
> again.

She was asking students to take dangerous steps: to let go of their
traditional ways of thinking, seeing, and operating in a classroom. In
the same way, she had allowed me to suggest changes that terrified
her. Just as she made herself accessible to her students as they practiced engaging with the readings rather than distancing from them
and as they practiced collaborating with and listening to one another,
she appreciated that I had been and could be right there to help her
as she fumbled with the new strategies for teaching:

> Like I really think the critical moment for me was the Walt
> Whitman poems last year. Do you remember that? And you
> said to ask them two things: "What does the poet feel, and
> how do you know?" From that moment I completely began
> to shift what I did. (March 22, 1990)

The Importance of
Continued Feedback for Reflection

The perspective that she felt our interactions had provided for her was not something she could "get" and then "have" permanently with no further doubts about her teaching. When I came to visit on April 27, 1990, my role was again that of reflecting back to her the positive things that had happened during the classes I had observed. By herself, she felt she could not change her tendency to generalize unhappily about the whole class from the few students who were not prepared or responding. My observing, reporting, and listening to her talk about that class helped her focus with clearer perspective on the whole and to see that it was, in fact, just a few in a given class who were not involved. "Sometimes," she said, "I don't notice until you're here."

She had cautioned me before I observed a certain class that it had become a hard one for her. Afterward, she reflected:

Maybe I was wrong about that, because they were great today. I think what's hard is that there's a segment that isn't prepared.

I feel like when you work the way I do, everyone has to be prepared. If people aren't, it messes things up, because they're waiting for me to tell them and I can't work that—I mean I don't want to do that. I mean I *will*, but I don't want to. It seems really stupid.

So I have to really make them be ready and some of them won't, but the majority is, and the majority is really doing their thing, because today they were great. I'm not going to say this was the best class, but this is pretty much how they are.

I guess I sometimes don't notice how hard my students work or how insightful they are. So maybe one of the things that's good for me is to have someone come in and watch the classes, that I also am more, I look at them more. I'm more conscious of what they're doing and how I'm facilitating that because I guess when you visit, that's sort of what I'm thinking about: what's happening in the classroom.

I guess I'm much more conscious of it because I know that's what we'll talk about, so I have to know. I think most days I go through the motions. We have the class but I don't really think about it. . . . I mean if it didn't go great I'm pretty conscious of it. But I'm probably more critical of how not good, I mean it's probably better than what I think.

Later in that same interview, I reported what I had seen in the class, validating her work:

Liz You gave them time to try to say what they needed to say.
Sheila Yeah.
Liz In both cases another kid said, "What he's trying to say . . ." or "What she's trying to say . . ." They really helped each other out . . .
Sheila Yeah.
Liz . . . because you had created some space.

Deep-seated issues kept arising as we worked. In November of 1989, still not sure whether the students could learn what they needed to learn in the situation she was setting up, Sheila was able to sort out the different aspects of her doubt: "They will make all the important points, I'm convinced of it, but they have to hear each other and they have to keep track of it."

As usual, she used our conversation as a way to create possibilities as she talked through the problem. Again she confirmed the pivotal importance of the chance to reflect with a listener:

I think it's hearing myself talk things through that makes it more clear, but doing it over and over again, I just know that I reached a point that I stepped over some line where I knew that it was—I felt in my gut, or my instinct, that this was going the way *I* want it to go. This feels good to me.

What I see my students doing is good work. They're thinking—and I'm talking 99% engagement here; I'm not talking 50, or 20. I'm talking high percentages. (March 20, 1990)

Change in Attitude

Sheila's more positive attitude about herself spilled over into seeing the good in other teachers. Working with them directly on the first Celebrate Education fair for the entire community and then on hosting the conference on heterogeneous grouping, Sheila expanded the range of her contacts with people who cared as passionately as she did about the children. Even though she still perceived a contradiction between what some teachers talked about and what they were actually doing, now that she was comfortable with herself, her tone consistently accepted herself as part of the faculty. The pronoun "I" began to be replaced by "we" as she talked about the struggle for change: "At least we're trying. We're a school that's trying and it's very hard. I mean it's not easy to change the way people have taught all their lives or to change the perception of what a school is" (March 20, 1990).

The same eager confidence, even excitement, about her students and her work carried through April 1990. She was working harder than ever but now the energy was consistently positive. After the school-hosted regional conference on heterogeneous grouping in mid-May, both Ralph and Ernest assured me that in spite of the budget cuts, Sheila would be rehired at the school committee meeting. Ernest invited Sheila out to a special lunch that he had once a month to honor students and teachers. She appeared on a video, promoting heterogeneous grouping and arguing passionately for teachers' work to be valued by the community. She liked herself when she played the video back:

> It's been a verifying week, that I'm really worth something. The video is me, my true self, sure of myself. For a long time I had lost my confidence. But I've begun to let go of the fear. In this last year I've felt all those things coming back! (June 12, 1990)

For Sheila as well as for her students what she said to me on the phone on May 21 was true: "I'm watching what can happen when people let themselves be who they are." Wanting her students to feel as empowered as she now did, she saw it happening: "That's what they're telling me: 'You give me a sense of confidence in myself. I can do things.' "

7 Reconceptualizing the Roles

Who Nurtures the Nurturers?

As she entered her position as English teacher at VCRHS, Sheila had been offered what seemed to be optimum conditions for success:

- Specifically having been hired to implement student-centered teaching in a small community school that had decided, with the encouragement of the school committee, to work toward heterogeneous grouping
- Administrative consciousness of the value of student-centeredness for students, and at least tacit commitment to trying to create it
- Some personal experience as a student in such a classroom as a balance to years of disempowering traditional schooling
- Enough years of experience with adolescents to be sure of her own delight in them, belief in their abilities, and assurance of their comfort with her
- Capacity for unrelenting hard work, for astonishingly clear organization, and for using resources imaginatively
- Strong academic and practical grounding in English, in curriculum development, and in special education

- Commitment to the growth of students for their own sake but also for the sake of a transformed world
- Unusual will, imagination, intelligence, and capacity for reflection

Even with all these advantages, Sheila's confidence was drained by internal and external pressures to doubt her pedagogical choices. Therefore, how much more would a teacher who did not start from such a strong foundation need support?

My presence for Sheila was a luxury that does not generally exist for classroom teachers. The outside help that she enjoyed and, in fact, according to Sheila, that was the catalyst for her full development as a student-centered teacher and mentor of other teachers attempting student-centered teaching is not generally available to induction-year teachers from the places that should have the greatest interest in and expertise about teaching (Grant & Zeichner, 1981). Unless practicing teachers are enrolled in graduate courses, they have little or no contact with teacher educators (Grant & Zeichner, 1981). Essentially, as teacher educators, we abandon our students once they graduate and/or are certified. Thus, it is no wonder that the absence of follow-up support by teacher educators results in predictable consequences for progressive and innovative teachers, who quickly become socialized to "the real world" of rather conservative perspectives that they find within the schools (Tabachnick & Zeichner, 1985; Wells, 1984). Unless teachers are very secure, in order to survive in that context, either they very quickly conform, internalizing the values of the culture or, ultimately, disappointed and frustrated, they leave teaching. Sheila was vacillating between those two choices until she gained the perspective provided by the mentoring.

It is tempting to be modest about the findings of this case study and conclude that Sheila was a very special person and the mentoring was a very special situation. I could cautiously refrain from suggesting that, with the kind of mentoring and advising that the research describes, all prospective or practicing teachers who choose to can become the kind of fully evolved student-centered teacher that I found Sheila to be well before the end of the study.

Although I am describing an exceptionally thoughtful, imaginative, energetic, and courageous teacher, I must also assert that just as student-centered teaching brings out the capacity for responsibility, creativity, independent thought, and full development in even the most unlikely students, the teacher-centered mentoring this book describes can bring out the positive attributes of teachers. In both cases, the crucial factor is the process of empowerment through support.

At the very least, the study allowed me to conclude that teachers who have the basic inner qualities to be drawn to doing this kind of work require, deserve, and can flourish with very careful, deliberate nurturing. There are many such teachers. I feel strongly now that the absence of such support has been the reason why there are so few student-centered teachers in our public schools. If such support were given to every teacher so identified, the shift toward a fully liberating education might very well take place.

Creating What We Need

As a teacher educator visiting schools looking for cooperating teachers who will model best practices, I have found that there is very little student-centered teaching going on within schools at any level, but especially in high schools. My experience confirms what the research shows: Actual teaching within schools has a conservative impact on new teachers, regardless of their incoming predispositions, ideals, or preservice training (Aaronsohn, 1988; Feiman-Nemser & Buchman, 1986; Tabachnick & Zeichner, 1985). Teacher educators like me are frustrated by the contradiction between what we send student teachers out to do and what they actually find themselves doing under the influence of even excellent cooperating teachers, whose practice reinforces traditional assumptions about teaching and learning.

That contradiction may, in part, account for some of the backlash against teacher preparation programs. In research studies, in popular accounts of how presumably useless preservice programs are, and in deeply ingrained attitudes of many practicing teachers, it is assumed that the progressive university is out of touch with "the real world." University teacher certification programs are characterized as having a love affair with "unrealistic" theories—such as engaging the students in text and in interaction and believing that a body of knowledge is less important than student construction of their own meaning.

The real world of high schools is understood to be a place in which the teachers, "in the trenches," pit themselves daily against reluctant students who resist being filled with certain required bodies of knowledge as well as against systems that interfere with good teaching but over which teachers are powerless. It seems to me that the business of preparing more people to be socialized into accepting that "real world" as normal or necessary is an illegitimate one.

On the other hand, as Sheila's experience indicates, it is unfair to send out preservice and new teachers with the expectation that their students and colleagues in those high schools or even elementary schools will welcome transformative student-centered teaching. Such expectations set them up for the kind of disillusionment that inevitably leads them to decide that "the research is wrong" and that traditional ways are the only ways that really work with their particular students or even with any students.

Being the only one in her school who felt and taught as she did isolated Sheila within her building, at least as she saw herself. My regular presence alone did not reassure her that her ideas were realistic for a high school; in fact, at first, associating with me actually removed her yet further from her peers, given how suspect university faculty are in secondary schools. She felt attacked by the pervasive argument that schools have no need of the fantasies spun in universities, nor time for reflection.

So what does that complex reality mean for the relevance of teacher education? Especially as standardized teacher competency tests drive programs to presocialize preservice teachers to the way things already are in the schools, it is clear that traditionally oriented schools will swallow up most temporarily idealistic new teachers unless we drastically reconceptualize the role and the program.

Zeichner and Liston's (1987) findings confirm what I have suspected from my own preservice teaching and student teacher supervision: It may not be possible to create a Sheila through a traditionally based teacher education program, but it is possible to cultivate, support, and sustain one within a nontraditional teacher education program. It might take more time, energy, and group support to bring to student-centeredness a teacher who did not start out with most of the professional and personal characteristics Sheila possessed, as listed previously. It took unusual will, imagination, intelligence, and sense of self for Sheila to begin to take the risk of letting go from within and resisting from without the more familiar and comfortable systems in which she had been trained and which predominated around her.

Zeichner and Liston (1987) point out, "To some extent we may be preparing student teachers for a teaching role that does not now exist, or does not have the sanction of the institutions in which teachers now work" (p. 44).

Clements (1975) prefigures Goodlad's (1990) call for "simultaneous renewal": "We cannot improve teacher education in isolation from the conduct of schooling. Improved teachers must go into existing schools" (p. 164).

Zeichner and Liston (1987) continue,

> More material and moral support must be given to the supervisors and teachers who work with our students. . . . And we need to work more closely with our colleagues outside of the School of Education so as to provide a greater continuity of experience for our students and the kinds of institutional support and structure which are consistent with our pedagogical goals. (p. 45)

They call for "strategies which seek to alter factors outside of the program's boundaries" (Zeichner & Liston, 1987, p. 45), strategies that will encourage both newly placed and veteran teachers to see themselves as agents of social change rather than as insignificant functionaries within overwhelming and inevitable systems.

This is a revolutionary call (Cagan, 1978; Freire, 1968; Rogers, 1977). It asks teachers, administrators, and students to consider challenging the notions of rugged individualism that isolate people from one another. Normally, nothing changes; teachers give up the innovation, or they give up teaching. As a result of generations in this cycle, teachers continue to be products of traditional schooling, trained to expect proper behavior and right answers from themselves and their students.

Even if they are drawn to challenge such narrow priorities, teachers will be confused by the combination of messages they hear. Teacher educators may speak of the whole child who learns by being active and interactive. They may speak of students making meaning within a complex social and political context. The culture of the high school, however, expects teachers to produce school-appropriate social and academic achievement represented essentially by student individualism and respect for the sole authorities of teacher and text.

A series of further questions arises from these contradictions. Who is there, regularly present but noninvested in the cultures of the schools, to help novice teachers internalize and retain the kind of perspective that will allow them to integrate the two agendas? Who is there to help teachers make a confident choice to swim against the tide by creating an environment in which students learn to make meaning from information and see others as resources, as opposed to accumulating an array of facts and proving they have mastered certain technical skills? Who is there in the schools to help teachers, along with their students, "learn to act and speak for themselves, help them gain control over the decisions affecting their daily lives" (Adams, 1972, p. 502; see also Combs, 1982)? Who is there to say it is good teaching to work this other way?

Implications for Teacher Educators

This case study describes an instance in which it is clear that regular, positive, nonevaluative, concrete feedback and opportunity for reflection supported a teacher through her struggle to sustain a vision that student-centered teaching can work and that students feel that they learn best when they construct their own knowledge. We know that not only by the report of the researcher but by the direct words of the teacher, her principal, some of her colleagues, and some of her students. Sheila is not the only high school teacher who needs, deserves, and would profit from the kind of support that this case study provided. In fact, the work of supporting Sheila, even in her traditional context, was relatively easy compared to the work of encouraging preservice student teachers and in-service teachers to persist in thinking of designing and implementing student-centered practices. To begin with, people who plan to be teachers have to experience student-centeredness for themselves if they are to come to believe in it. So we have to model it in our teacher education courses, consciously and pervasively. As uncomfortable as it will be for university students to shift from being passive and individualistic receivers of knowledge to becoming active, collaborative participants in their own learning, that very discomfort can serve as powerful information on which to reflect in a deep and sustained way about the legacy of traditional schooling.

We have to let people about to be teachers practice figuring out what is important in text, perhaps for the first time in their lives. We must require that they get a healthy dose of practice in designing and implementing student-centered rather than teacher-centered or content-centered mini-lessons (reflective teaching) within our class-rooms. They must directly experience and get feedback on keeping themselves out of the center of their lessons. We can say to them and to the student teachers we supervise, "I will see *one* 'direct instruction' lesson, to prove you can do it. After that, all the rest have to be student centered: no lecturing and no answer-pulling."

In order to see one another as resources rather than as rivals, preservice teachers have to experience noncompetitiveness, and constant practice in the social skills of collaboration and conflict management, in our teacher education classrooms. We have to let them dialogue intensively about how they see the teaching role: In particular, how do they feel when people they are responsible for are in struggle? Perhaps all of the issues Sheila raised can come to light in a university classroom, especially if we make room for that to happen. Our university students must see their professors give up both teacher-centeredness and content-centeredness. When they experience us not as experts but as facilitators of their learning, they will be more likely to see themselves in that transformed role with their students.

Critical Junctures

Student Teaching. All the work we do in certification courses at the university could be a blip on their screens, however, if preservice teachers who come out of challenging courses ready to apply their new philosophies find themselves in classrooms of cooperating teachers who do not believe such practices will "work." From my observation of student teachers in their placements, from my conversations with them before and after those observations, and from my collection of preservice teacher writings, I see people learning to be teachers trapped between university ideals and the dominant—though often unconscious—traditional "institutional realities" within the schools and within themselves. A student teacher from one of my early certification courses wrote,

> I found myself lecturing to make sure I covered as much information as possible. I felt I was being remiss in my duties if I didn't cover every agency that FDR ever created. The students were bored by this but I felt they had to have it.

But they liked the group-oriented projects the best. I
should have used more of those. They liked the way I was
involved with them, related to them, genuinely cared about
them. (Mark, 1988)

Another student teacher whom I had worked with in several
courses spoke of a struggle, mostly within himself, that he had not
anticipated until he was actually teaching:

Do I believe in cooperative learning? Will they talk to each
other? What if the text *doesn't* raise any questions? Where do
they find answers? The other teachers are dentists—answer
pullers! How do I exist in their system?

She evaluated me on how I controlled the class—on who
was off-task. She focused on one group that was negative.
How am I going to make the school people happy? Give
multiple choice tests?

I'm stuck for ideas for cooperative projects, and I have
[my university history professor] on my shoulder, saying,
"You don't know any history." What should I do? (Al, 1991)

Another used our postobservation conference to gain perspective on her own confusion of values:

When [my cooperating teacher] says "they can't" so much, I
tend to fall into her way of thinking. (Cari, 1991)

Yet another found value in just being heard by a teacher educator
who shared her vision:

I've been trying to sort all the issues out. . . . It's been so good
to talk. (Elyse, 1989)

Still another, a former student I was not supervising, came to my
office:

I just need a reality check—I need to know I'm not crazy; this
stuff *does* work with kids, right? (Margie, 1995)

These are the successes. The evidence of this case study confirms other indications that teachers who would otherwise take creative risks get stuck in traditional approaches because of the absence of opportunity for ongoing dialogue about the choices they are making (Bussis et al., 1976; Goodlad, 1990; Sarason, 1982). It is best if the dialogue is with a person knowledgeable about and committed to alternative pedagogy. When teachers immediately process classroom events with a teacher educator or colleague who advocates student-centered learning, they are reminded to think in terms of pairing or grouping their students. One student teacher's comments reflect Sheila's—and many other teachers' and student teachers'—reactions to direct observation-based feedback:

> Seeing my cooperating teacher every day, and especially having her *approve* of my lecturing and answer pulling, has made it hard for me to remember what I really had wanted to be doing in my classes.
>
> You were my conscience: Having you come in made me examine my assumptions and shook me out of that comfortable place of her approval. (Al, March 12, 1991)

Traditionally taught courses do not give student teachers what they need beyond the peer interaction that is often more valuable than the course material. What teachers need beyond the short-term group experience of those courses is sustained, on-site support for development. The key person here, therefore, is the university supervisor of student teaching. A supervisor knowledgeable about and committed to student-centered teaching can try to persuade a traditional cooperating teacher at least to allow the student teacher the freedom to explore and practice what she or he learned at the university. Many of the people playing the role of supervisor, however, seem to be adjunct faculty, often retired teachers, whose concept of good teaching tends to be quite traditional and who encourage the student teachers they supervise to play that role. It is heartbreaking to hear from student teachers I taught but did not supervise that they did not want to rock any boats by trying strategies that were not already in place.

My experience as well as that of many student teachers I have observed in their placements is that under the best of circumstances, it may take at least 6 weeks for a teacher committed to student-centered teaching to bring a class through a full transition from a teacher-centered to a student-centered classroom. Knowing that, I am sadly amused when I hear a teacher or student teacher say, "I tried it once, and it didn't work, so I went back to regular teaching."

Alone in Their Own Classrooms. In the normal course of events, most student teachers, at a point well before the end of the semester, long for their own classrooms, confident that all they need is autonomy. The reckoning comes once they have their own classrooms. They are no longer guests in someone else's space, trying themselves out with someone else's students and subject to the judgment of someone with power over their grade and perhaps skeptical of their pedagogical choices. Do they now have freedom? More important, perhaps, do they feel they do?

Teacher education programs operate on the assumption that if a preservice teacher has many university courses that model, discuss, observe, and require the practice of excellent teaching, and especially if that preservice teacher has a university supervisor knowledgeable about, supportive of, and expecting excellent teaching, he or she will be in good shape for the induction year of teaching. However, my own expectation that that would be so was challenged by the case of Josh, whom I had taught in two certification courses, who did research with me, and whose brilliant, completely student-centered student teaching I had personally supervised.

Believing that he of all people would be fine in his own classroom, being preoccupied with my regular faculty responsibilities and courses of the new semester, and, above all, forgetting what I had learned from the beginning of my intensive 2 years with Sheila, I decided to give Josh time to establish a relationship with his new students before I checked in. When I finally called in October or later, and then visited him in his own first classroom, I found him frustrated, unhappy, and overwhelmed.

The pressure he was feeling to cover a districtwide curriculum had him resenting the large number of special needs children in his room. Focusing on his own need to achieve what he felt was expected of him, he blamed them for impeding him. Too late, I recognized his great anxiety about "wasting time" by backing up to allow the children to arrive at competence before going on with where he wanted—or felt he needed—to be in the book. His words sadly reminded me of the reaction of one traditional high school teacher whom I had interviewed about his reluctance to use cooperative learning: "Time!" this teacher had insisted. "My class time is too precious. We can't waste class time with it. We have so much information to cover. I haven't got the time to set them up and follow them through" (1987).

In addition to forgetting Sheila, I had also forgotten three other factors:

1. That our certification program required only one course in special education
2. That although during his preparation periods he had volunteered and taught beautifully in a special education resource room, Josh's student teaching had been within a rigidly tracked system. Thus, he had had no experience with managing heterogeneity
3. How frequently I had heard both student teachers and new practicing teachers, not yet trusting their own professional judgment, say, as Sheila had, that they thought they "had to" do what seemed to be expected of them

A Model From Beyond Our Borders

The gap in support for Josh in this case strongly reinforced my sense that teacher education programs abandon our preservice teachers at the most vulnerable time—transition from the rather nurturing environment of the university and the cooperating teacher's classroom to the isolation of their own. At best, the usual procedure in the United States has been either to consider the certified teacher an essentially finished product who may or may not choose to come back to the university for further credits, or to require graduate courses leading toward an advanced degree. These courses are often seen as more of the same—lectures or at best seminars at the university.

The perspective in Australia seems more enlightened. There, induction year teachers are considered to be at their "ultimate teaching moment," fully eligible for mentoring by an assistance committee, which includes a professor of teacher education (Andrews, 1987, p. 143). What Australians call "entry-year" is seen as a developmental phase in teacher education along the continuum of ongoing professional development of teachers, separate from supervision (Andrews, 1987).

The Australian program is grounded in the belief that "not all teachers will lose their idealism or experience transitional shock during their first year of teaching if supportive and respectful teaching environments are present" (Andrews, 1987, p. 148). When the school context includes active and supportive staff development, beginning teachers can innovate. They need not merely succumb to "socialized compliance" or be overwhelmed by regulations and expectations (Andrews, 1987, p. 148).

Teachers there, it is assumed, need to experiment under "relatively safe conditions" with a mentor who shares a compatible teaching orientation. Far from the role of facilitating assimilation, the Australian mentor's job is to keep the new teacher from being too cautious (Andrews, 1987, pp. 149-152). Essentially alone with a difficult group of children, Josh, as well as others, certainly could have profited from the support of such a program. Like most people in new situations, he had not yet, in his first vulnerable year, figured out which "requirements" were real and which were guidelines subject to a teacher's professional judgment.

Even long-term veteran teachers, going through changes as we hope all teachers will, can desperately need support. For example, Joe and Lois, whom I happened on in their respective schools, felt validated, encouraged, and reenergized by my enthusiasm for their exciting attempts at student-centered teaching within traditional schools. We confirmed those relationships of support and mutual learning by my bringing university students each semester to see student-centered teaching in action, and by their reciprocal visits as guest speakers in my classes. Both veteran teachers have periodically indicated, as Sheila had, that without my encouragement they would have reverted to former, easier methods, or quit teaching.

Joe and Lois continue to use our visits, conversations, and ongoing dialogue with one another, with Josh, and with teacher education students as opportunities to reflect, rethink, and recommit to their choices. Although they happen with less frequency than those I enjoyed with Sheila, these connections have been as important to my teaching as they seem to have been to theirs.

Because I found Sheila, Joe, and Lois totally by chance, operating in isolation in very different schools in widely divergent socio-

economic situations, I am convinced that such teachers are every-
where, working courageously and innovatively, and very much in
need of connection with teacher educators who believe in them and,
as they do, in their students.

The Issue of Labor-Intensiveness

Until institutions in the United States decide to learn from the
Australian model, it will be necessary to find ways to provide support for student-centered teaching whenever a teacher in struggle
like Sheila exists. Although the one-on-one relationship that I had
with her may be the ideal, the approach used in the 2-year study that
this book documents may be prohibitively labor-intensive, especially
if one considers the significant numbers of student teachers and practicing teachers who need and deserve support.

How is it possible to achieve that kind of frequency of visits and
conversations and that intense focus on one individual teacher? Is
that much work necessary? How might such efforts be made more
economical and thus cost-effective? Is it possible to think about cost-
effectiveness and still provide the intensive, sustained feedback and
reflection that this study describes and finds necessary?

First, it is important to say that if there is another teacher out there
like Sheila—and there are others—this much effort is worth it.
Teacher educators may then decide within their own program and
its constraints and possibilities to take some or all of the following
steps once they identify a teacher like Sheila, committed to the struggle toward student-centeredness:

- Learn from her or him what is possible in immediate real-life
  classrooms.
- Send or bring preservice and in-service teachers to observe her
  or his classes.
- Invite her or him to be a cooperating teacher and to coteach or
  at least be a guest teacher of teacher education courses or
  teacher-in-residence for a period of time.
- Do participatory research with her or him on issues that arise
  from her or his teaching.
- Cowrite for journals that practicing teachers read.
- Work with her or him to write grants to restructure the school
  in which she or he works to allow teachers within it release

time to observe in one another's classes and give feedback to one another.

- If the teacher education program is too far away from the university for students to observe or student teach with her or him, videotape the classes, focusing on students rather than on her or him as a teacher. Use those videos in teacher education courses to stimulate dialogue about how teachers get themselves there. Bring in the teacher as facilitator of that conversation after the viewing. Get the videos onto mainstream TV specials as models of excellence, challenging the usual ones that are driven by the dynamic personality of one unique but almost always traditional teacher.

- Help her or him network with others who share the same vision. Models exist for support groups of such teachers from different schools coming together regularly, often over dinner, with a teacher educator as convener and facilitator to share their struggles and brainstorm possibilities (Williams & Williamson, 1994). That group may have had its origins in a student-centered university teacher certification course in which preservice teachers have already done the bonding and trust building that such a group requires. With institutional support from their respective schools, these group members could usefully visit one another's classrooms on a rotating basis to get and give direct, concrete feedback. They can start by staying in regular touch by phone and E-mail, bolstering one another's spirits. It is important to know they are not alone.

- Stay in constant touch by phone and through E-mail, with the teacher educator and/or with the support group.

- Above all, learn from her or him.

- Be there. Don't let her or him quit teaching.

It is true that the kind of mentoring that Sheila experienced from a teacher educator took an enormous amount of time and attention. In fact, it would be easy to say that if the intensive work described in this book had not been a research investigation, it would not have taken place. Nevertheless, that kind of intensive, frequent contact can sometimes be called for in effective supervision of student teachers. Therefore, before dismissing this structure as an unrealistic model for mentoring of practicing teachers, three aspects of the investigation would be important for teacher educators, school administrators, and school committees to notice.

First, apart from the time spent in the transcribing, storing, organizing, and analyzing of the data—work that a researcher would do in any situation—all of the time invested in the mentoring except for the driving was as professionally beneficial to the teacher educator as it was to the teacher. I did not need to "prepare" in the traditional sense, although my ongoing reading was useful for our conversations. I was there to be alert, observant, and open. By practicing active listening with Sheila, I became a much better active listener and clinical supervisor for my student teachers in their placements. Working with Sheila made me sensitive to teachers' fears, and helped me let go of the supervisor posture that can get in the way of trust. Far from detracting from my own teaching, the privilege of such frequent, intensive witnessing of high school lessons and interactions, and such an in-depth view of a teacher's daily as well as long-range struggle to teach well, gave substance and credibility to my own work with preservice and other in-service teachers. Perhaps it would be a refreshing sabbatical project for a university professor.

Second, the situation thus described seems to call for the regular, active, and carefully negotiated presence of teacher educators in the schools as mutually respectful partners with practicing teachers. If John Goodlad's (1990) conception of simultaneous renewal begins to receive widespread practice, teacher educators will be routinely spending much of their time inside the schools. They will supervise cohorts of student teachers and work directly with practicing teachers as colleagues. Extending that colleagueship over student teachers to conversation about and actual feedback on the work of some of those practicing teachers who desire it is a logical next step. Goodlad's model assumes the value of close, respectful, mutually supportive relationships between teacher educators and classroom teachers. In addition, the availability of the teacher educator on-site will make it possible to break some of the isolation of teachers from one another even if the work cannot always be as one-on-one as this study was.

On-site on a regular basis, teaching and often coteaching the university preservice secondary courses right there at the high school, teacher educators would be easily available as both equals with and advisers to practicing teachers, many but not necessarily all of whom would be the cooperating teachers of the cadre of student teachers.

The main attribute of the new role, like the role of the student-centered teacher, is that of a resource person who listens respectfully as a teacher/learner rather than expert or critic (Adams & Horton, 1975; Bussis et al., 1976; Freire, 1968). The role would be to model and then facilitate the process of being present with teachers who request nonevaluative concrete feedback and opportunity for reflection.

Third, if Sheila was telling the truth about herself, the mentoring she received kept her in teaching. If we are as serious as we say we are as a nation about wanting to attract to and retain within the teaching profession people who think hard, well, divergently, and imaginatively; who care about and attend to the whole student; who are willing to live with uncertainty if they can see that their risks might benefit the students; if, in other words, we really want to populate our schools with change agents, the time and energy that this kind of support work requires is a cost worth paying.

To do the work of mentoring a teacher like Sheila, teacher educators will be most effective who are knowledgeable about student-centered teaching and cooperative learning strategies, about a range of divergent ways of seeing and knowing, and about the practice of active listening. In terms of the academic content, it was helpful to Sheila that I had in my own teaching of English already figured out how I felt about most of the traditional agenda items. On the other hand, as I told Sheila in the last few months of the study, I was learning more from her about how to teach English well than I had ever thought of when I was doing it myself. Having supervised student teachers in all academic subject areas, I feel confident that, just as a student-centered teacher leaves the struggle with a text to her students, a mentor can confidently work with a teacher without being an expert in that teacher's subject area. The process is the important content in both student-centered teaching and in mentoring.

Reflection. Well after the trust between us had been solidly built, Sheila said, "Being the object of such scrutiny definitely makes me think about what I'm doing, which is missing for teachers."

What does it mean if teachers, after the initial anxiety of beginning, have very little occasion to think with another about what they are doing? The Connecticut State Department of Education (1989) expects of mentor teachers and cooperating teachers that they will "have regular dialogues with their beginning or student teachers about the teaching process," because "opportunities to reflect about teaching with colleagues are rare, and beginning teachers report that such opportunities are invaluable" (p. 2).

In both K-12 schools and universities, teachers dialogue with students more than with colleagues, but both are crucial for teachers' growth. Teachers need the support of fellow professionals in times of doubt and confusion. They also need the stimulation of ideas, the fulfillment of interacting, and the perspective that comes only with feedback and with believing in long-range evidence that they have made a difference (Combs, 1982).

In the suggested evolving and interactive new roles for teacher educators (Bussis et al., 1976; Sergiovanni & Starratt, 1979), it is necessary to start where people are. As in all teaching, we need to work out certain problems having to do with habits of fierce individualism, competitiveness, and lack of institutional commitment, left over from the traditional assumptions held by most teachers, teacher educators, and administrators (Ruddick, 1987; Wideen & Andrews, 1987). The opportunity for all participants, including the teacher educators, is to develop ways to receive and give support in the ongoing effort, which Sheila described simply as "becoming a better teacher." Ultimately, the very process by which teachers become better at what they do will have created the kind of collaboration, cooperation, partnership, mutuality, collegiality, and interactive development that characterizes effective schools (Goodlad, 1990; Wideen & Andrews, 1987).

Implementing What We Know

Based on what I have learned from the study, I think teacher educators should begin by simply spending much more time in schools. If we are to find out how their theories play out in practice, we must observe in depth and over time what happens when teachers of unusual vision find themselves in conflict with traditional structures. This case study suggests the complexity of the situation and the need for what Sheila called a constant reminder of what she started out to do. Especially if they hope to make a difference in that process, teacher educators must decide to do what practicing teachers keep asking us to do: move outside the walls of colleges and universities. Even longer range, if we hope to participate in the kind

of total change that Goodlad (1990) refers to as "simultaneous renewal" of education and teacher education, we might consider locat-
ing at least part of our preparatory programs in the public schools
themselves.

The question of the role and even the identity of teacher educators arises as small colleges and, in periods of political or economic
retrenchment, even larger colleges and universities turn over the
teaching of secondary classroom methods courses to professors of
academic subjects. Such faculty may be excellent at their subject areas
and even in the craft of teaching, but they are generally not grounded
in the secondary school experience. What realistic expectation can
there be that they will welcome spending time in the schools or that
their feedback on teaching methods will be useful to teachers of adolescents? Can we expect that they would be helpful to teachers who
would like to experiment with student-centered approaches? Before
characterizing them as completely content-centered but also before
engaging them for secondary methods courses, it would be useful to
investigate the extent to which college teachers of academic subjects
have thought and studied about complex issues of pedagogy, or are
willing not only to do so but also to model student-centeredness in
their own teaching. Some colleges and universities are encouraging
their own faculties to engage in "relearning" or such other dialogues
on pedagogy. Frequently, these emerge naturally out of efforts to
create interdisciplinary courses, especially in small colleges.

From the twin questions "Who nurtures the nurturers?" and
"Who should mentor?" emerges a new issue: "Who should be the
teacher educators if research-based practices such as student-
centered teaching are to be infused into school systems of the future?"
Except for some on the early childhood and early elementary level,
most teachers who are presently operating student-centered classrooms report that they started out as traditional teachers, both
teacher- and content-centered. That finding should serve (a) as a reminder that teacher educators also may very well still be tied to traditional assumptions about teaching and (b) as evidence that people
can change. The question most usefully addressed might be, "What
were the forces that initiated, encouraged, and sustained your new
choices?" The findings of this study suggest that the very asking of
those questions by a researcher knowledgeable about and positive
about the value of student-centered teaching might encourage teach-

ers to continue reflecting on their own choices, thereby supporting reaffirmed commitment to their enlarged vision.

As an extension of those questions, it would be useful to understand what teacher education programs expect of teacher educators and how teacher educators are prepared. Beyond research, scholarship, professional service, advising, and the teaching of courses, the already labor-intensive but crucial work of teacher educators is supervision: being in classrooms with individual student teachers and helping them reflect about their experiences. The kind of support of practicing teachers that this study recommends is essentially an effective but nonevaluative supervision relationship.

How do people learn how to do the kind of supporting that people like Sheila need? Most teacher education programs assume that if a person has taught successfully in a public school, that person is automatically qualified to supervise student teachers. I have learned this to be not necessarily true. Whether full-time faculty, adjuncts, or graduate assistants are employed as supervisors of student teachers, systematic efforts must be made to help supervisors think about the work they do. Beyond readings or courses, regular dialogues about what constitutes good teaching should be a part of what is offered to people who are observing, giving feedback, and, in most cases, evaluating classroom performance. Such dialogues will provide opportunity to reflect on their own expectations, in small groups with other supervisors who may or may not share their assumptions.

Attention must be paid to how the cognitive dissonance that thus arises is handled. Role-plays, simulations, and other activities should be part of the preparation and support of prospective and practicing supervisors to help them develop skills of active listening. In order to maximize effectiveness, a match could be made carefully between student teachers who think they might want to do student-centered work and supervisors who will respect and can extend that work. This is especially important if the cooperating teachers within the school buildings have not had experience with or interest in pedagogies other than the traditional teacher- and content-centered ones.

It will be necessary to identify processes for approaching entrenched college professors, especially teacher educators, with invitations to consider reconceptualizing their assumptions about their own roles. Even though they might espouse theories of alternative pedagogies, do they themselves trust those theories and their students enough to actually practice them, and thus have their students experience their power? Are they themselves ready to let go of content-centeredness?

Teacher educators, like school teachers, need perspective on their own and one another's assumptions and belief systems about teaching and learning (Munby, 1982) and their own teaching effectiveness, but may not have satisfying ways to gain it. Special education teachers, early childhood teachers, and teacher educators often have ideas about cooperative learning and classroom environments that general education faculty might not have had occasion to study in depth. Regular, sustained, collaborative reflection beyond artificial departmental boundaries should be as useful to teacher educators as it is to teachers.

The same questions that emerged from the study of a high school are salient here. Do institutions of higher learning provide or value that expenditure of faculty time (Sorcinelli, 1978)? Are professors likely to be initially fearful or suspicious of attention to their assumptions and exposure of their uncertainties? Would they fear the presence of a colleague in their classrooms? Might fear of judgment and resistance to change inhibit transformation of education at the college level as surely as it does at the secondary level? Without transformed college teaching, can it be reasonably expected that secondary teaching will change? Where must the cycle begin?

The questions that must be asked about the mentoring of high school teachers must also be asked at the postsecondary level. If teachers at the college/university level might profit from supportive interventions, who should do that mentoring/advising? I have begun to experience colleagues informally but quite effectively visiting one another's classrooms and giving valuable in-depth feedback for one another, so perhaps that mentor does not need to be, as Sheila found, an outside person with classroom and research credibility but with no investment in the politics of that particular department or institution. Can college professors overcome their own defensiveness? What institutional structures need to change and what support and relearning need to take place for that to happen? Does a mentor from either inside or outside have enough interest, knowledge, and commitment to spend time in the classrooms of colleagues? Would the faculty trust such a person? How would it "count," and who would pay?

It is important that a mentor give consistent, unhurried presence and attention to "the concrete situations in the classroom"

(Katz et al., 1974, p. 157). Such unhurried presence allows the mentor to serve as personal and professional support through the uncomfortable period of change (Katz et al., 1974). Ultimately, can a transitional outside mentor serve to bring the faculty together over time until they become resources for one another?

Perhaps what is necessary is to locate and encourage as teacher educators people who are ready to model student-centered teaching, and to provide opportunities for students to practice it and talk about it. One immediate place to look is among the increasing numbers of people who are educating themselves and others about multicultural and diversity education. In advocating full inclusion of women, people of color, and others whose voices have been unrepresented within the dominant curriculum (Adams & Horton, 1975; Banks, 1975; Belenky et al., 1986; Freire, 1968), they speak of transformed process as well as transformed content. They recommend cooperative and other interactive, student-centered learning as strategies most conducive to a full experience for all students of the multiple realities of an increasingly diverse and richly complex world.

Conclusion

In the spring of the first year of the data gathering, I berated myself for not being more systematic in rehearing and rethinking my data as I went along, and for not reading more widely between visits. I wanted to be more useful to Sheila each time we met together. My full-time work as a teacher educator—teaching, advising, committees, research—got in the way of my doing this support work as I thought I should.

What I came to realize, however, was that the real usefulness of my role was not that of the well-prepared expert, but that of active listener and friend. Sheila did most of the work and, therefore, most of the growing. As I watched Sheila over the 2 years, I realized that like a gardener, the student-centered teacher—and teacher educator—prepares a rich, basic environment, settles the seedlings carefully, goes up and down among the plants to make sure they are not being crowded, and restirs and nurtures the soil. Then, warily watching the sky, she steps back and lets natural processes work.

Operational Definitions

TRADITIONAL TEACHING

Any teaching in which the focus is on the content, about which the teacher is understood to be expert, and which must be "covered" in such a way that students will be able to show that they have acquired a certain body of knowledge. Student activity is that of watching and listening to the teacher. Students speak when called on in response to teacher questions. Student conversation with other students is generally unauthorized.

STUDENT-CENTERED TEACHING

Any teaching in which the focus is not on the teacher as performer, rescuer, or repository of wisdom, nor on the content as given material that must be covered, but on students' interaction with accessible, meaningful content, with one another, and with the teacher as facilitator of that interdependence. Process is an essential part of the content in this form of instruction.

177

SUPPORTING

1. A colleague's active listening[1] to a teacher as he or she talks through whatever he or she is feeling about his or her teaching, punctuated by statements or questions designed to open options when thinking seems to get stuck
2. Responding to direct requests for help with lessons or classroom management, brainstorming interactive lessons together, co-planning cooperative learning events, and helping analyze the teacher's effectiveness
3. Being in the classroom frequently, seeing what the teacher sees but with a different perspective, and naming what the observer sees
4. Being available at the school or on the telephone for conversations before and after the scheduled observations
5. Helping the teacher focus on the positive things that happen as opposed to what does not happen
6. Letting the teacher know what other people in the same situation are thinking about and doing. Decreasing the sense of isolation by helping establish a network with teachers in other schools whose vision and struggle are similar
7. Validating what the teacher does well
8. At the teacher's request, demonstrating the possibilities

Note

1. *Active listening* is a term understood by psychologists to mean listening with full, respectful attention. The listener encourages and clarifies by reflecting back what has been heard, without judgment or interpretation (Faber & Mazlish, 1980; Ginott, 1965; Gordon, 1974; Rogers, 1951).

Resources on
Student-Centered Teaching

Aaronsohn, E. N. (1986a). *The changer and the changed.* Unpublished manuscript.

Aaronsohn, E. N. (1986b). *Collaboration as a subversive activity.* Unpublished manuscript.

Aaronsohn, E. N. (1987). *What can happen when you're real with kids.* Unpublished manuscript.

Aaronsohn, E. N. (1988). *The process is the content: The reluctance of high school teachers to use cooperative learning.* Unpublished comprehensive examination, University of Massachusetts at Amherst.

Aaronsohn, E. N., & Fischetti, J. A. (1990). Collaboration starts inside schools of education: Teacher educators as collaborators. In H. Schwartz (Ed.), *Collaboration: Building common agendas* (pp. 138-144). New York: Teachers College Press.

Ashton-Warner, S. (1963). *Teacher.* New York: Simon & Schuster.

Bell, L., & Schniedewind, N. (1986). *Reflective minds/intentional hearts: Joining humanistic education and critical theory for liberating education.* New Paltz: State University of New York.

Brandes, D., & Ginnis, P. (1986). *A guide to student-centered learning.* Oxford, England: Basil Blackwell.

Bricker-Jenkins, M., & Hooyman, N. (1987). Feminist pedagogy in education for social change. *Feminist Teacher, 2*(2), 36-42.

Britzman, D. P. (1988). On educating the educators. *Harvard Educational Review, 58*(1), 85-94.

diBenedetto, A. (1988). *The disempowerment of youth.* Unpublished comprehensive examination, University of Massachusetts at Amherst.

Dienhart, P. (1988). The active learning alternative. *Update, 15*(4), 5-6.

Dienhart, P., & Shepherd, N. (1988). Cooperation in the classroom. *Update, 15*(4), 6-7.

Duke, D. (1986). Understanding what it means to be a teacher. *Educational Leadership, 44*(2), 26-32.

Elder, J. M. (1974). *Distancing behaviors among white groups dealing with racism.* Unpublished manuscript, University of Connecticut School of Social Work.

Fader, D. (1976). *The new hooked on books.* New York: Berkeley Books.

Feiman-Nemser, S., & Buchman, M. (1986). *Knowing, thinking and doing in learning to teach: A research framework and some initial results.* East Lansing: Michigan State University, Institute for Research on Teaching.

Fischetti, J. A., & Santilli, S. (1988). *The mask of teacher education reform.* Amherst: University of Massachusetts, Math English Science Technology Education Project (MESTEP).

Glassman, P. (1988, April). *A study of cooperative learning in mathematics, writing, and reading as implemented in third, fourth, and fifth grade classes: A focus upon achievement, attitudes, and self-esteem for males, females, blacks, Hispanics, and Anglos.* Paper presented at the annual meeting of the American Educational Research Association, New Orleans, LA.

Goodman, J. (1987, April). *Key factors in becoming (or not becoming) an empowered elementary school teacher: A preliminary study of selected novices.* Paper presented at the annual meeting of the American Educational Research Association, Washington, DC.

Gordon, A. B. (1985). *Cooperative learning: A comparative study of attitude and achievement of two groups of grade 7 mathematics classes.* Unpublished doctoral dissertation, Brigham Young University, Utah.

Grant, J. (1987). The dynamics of the women's studies classroom. *Radical Teacher, 22,* 24.

Holt Associates. *Growing without schooling* [Newsletter]. Cambridge, MA: Author.

Jenkins, L., & Kramer, C. (1978). Small group process: Learning from women. *Women's Studies International Quarterly, 1*(1), 67-84.

Lewis, M., & Simon, R. I. (1986). A discourse not intended for her: Learning and teaching within patriarchy. *Harvard Educational Review, 56*(4), 457-472.

McIntosh, P. (1983). *Interactive phases of curricular revision: A feminist perspective.* Wellesley, MA: Wellesley College Center for Research on Women.

Nederhood, B. (1986). *The effects of student team learning on academic achievement, attitudes toward self and school, and expansion of friendship bonds among middle school students.* Unpublished doctoral dissertation, University of Washington, Seattle.

Schaef, A. W. (1986). *Codependence misunderstood—mistreated.* San Francisco: Harper & Row.

Slavin, R. (1983). *Cooperative learning.* New York: Longman.

Slavin, R. (1985). *Learning to cooperate, cooperating to learn.* New York: Plenum.

Stitzel, J. (1988). Unlearning not to speak: Feminism in the classroom. *Frontiers: A Journal of Women's Studies, 4*(1), 47-49.

Wilkinson, L. C., & Dollaghan, C. (1978). Peer communication in first-grade reading groups. *Theory Into Practice, 18*(4), 267-274.

References

Aaronsohn, E. (1988). *The process is the content.* Unpublished manuscript and annotated bibliography, University of Massachusetts at Amherst.

Adams, F. (1972). Highlander Folk School: Getting information, going back and teaching it. *Harvard Educational Review, 42*(4), 497-520.

Adams, F. W., & Horton, M. (1975). *Unearthing seeds of fire: The idea of Highlander.* Winston-Salem, NC: John T. Blair.

Andrews, I. (1987). Induction programs: Staff development opportunities for beginning and experienced teachers. In M. F. Wideen & I. Andrews (Eds.), *Staff development for school improvement: A focus on the teacher* (pp. 143-152). New York: Falmer.

Aronson, E. (1978). *The jigsaw classroom.* Beverly Hills, CA: Sage.

Ashton-Warner, S. (1963). *Teacher.* New York: Simon & Schuster.

Avila, D. L., Combs, A. W., & Purkey, W. W. (Eds.). (1973). *The helping relationship sourcebook.* Boston: Allyn & Bacon.

Banks, J. A. (1975). *Teaching strategies for ethnic studies.* Boston: Allyn & Bacon.

Belenky, M. F., Clinchy, B. M., Goldberger, N. R., & Tarule, J. M. (1986). *Women's ways of knowing: The development of self, voice, and mind.* New York: Basic Books.

Bezucha, R. J. (1985). Feminist pedagogy as a subversive activity. In M. Culley & C. Portuges (Eds.), *Gendered subjects: The dynamics of feminist teaching* (pp. 81-95). Boston: Routledge Kegan Paul.

Blase, J. J. (1987). The politics of teaching: The teacher-parent relationship and the dynamics of diplomacy. *Journal of Teacher Education, 38,* 53-60.

Blase, J. J. (1988). The everyday political perspective of teachers: Vulnerability and conservatism. *Qualitative Studies in Education, 2*(2), 125-142.

Bowles, S., & Gintis, H. (1976). *Schooling in capitalist America: Educational reform and the contradictions of economic life.* New York: Basic Books.

Britzman, D. P. (1985). *Reality and ritual: An ethnographic study of student teachers.* Unpublished doctoral dissertation, University of Massachusetts School of Education at Amherst.

Bussis, A. M., Chittenden, E. A., & Amarel, M. (1976). *Beyond surface curriculum.* Boulder, CO: Westview.

Cagan, E. (1978). Individualism, collectivism, and radical educational reform. *Harvard Educational Review, 48*(2), 227-251.

Callahan, R. E. (1962). *Education and the cult of efficiency: A study of the social forces that have shaped the administration of the public schools.* Chicago: University of Chicago Press.

Carey, L. M., & Marsh, D. D. (1980). *University roles in inservice education: Planning for change.* Washington, DC: American Association of Colleges of Teacher Education.

Clements, M. (1975). Alternatives in teacher education curriculum theory. *Network, 5,* 161-167.

Collins, J. L., & Seidman, I. E. (1980). Language and secondary schooling: The struggle for meaning. *English Education, 12,* 5-9.

Combs, A. W. (1982). *A personal approach to teaching: Beliefs that make a difference.* Boston: Allyn & Bacon.

Connecticut State Department of Education. (1989, Summer). *Update,* p. 2.

Cormier, R. (1977). *I am the cheese.* New York: Pantheon.

Cormier, R. (1988). *Fade.* New York: Delacorte.

Culley, M., Diamond, A., Edwards, L., Lennox, S., & Portuges, C. (1985). The politics of nurturance. In M. Culley & C. Portuges (Eds.), *Gendered subjects: The dynamics of feminist teaching* (pp. 11-20). Boston: Routledge Kegan Paul.

Culley, M., & Portuges, C. (Eds.). (1985). *Gendered subjects: The dynamics of feminist teaching.* Boston: Routledge Kegan Paul.

Dewey, J. (1974a). The school and society. In R. D. Archambault (Ed.), *John Dewey on education* (pp. 295-310). Chicago: University of Chicago Press. (Original work published 1899)

Dewey, J. (1974b). The relation of theory to practice in education. In R. D. Archambault (Ed.), *John Dewey on education* (pp. 313-338). Chicago: University of Chicago Press. (Original work published 1904)

Elbow, P. (1981). *Writing with power.* New York: Oxford University Press.

Faber, A., & Mazlish, E. (1980). *How to talk so kids will listen and listen so kids will talk.* New York: Avon.

Feiman-Nemser, S., & Buchman, M. (1986). *When is student teaching teacher education?* East Lansing: Michigan State University, Institute for Research on Teaching.

Floden, R. E., & Clark, C. (1988). Preparing teachers for uncertainty. *Teachers College Record, 89*(4), 505-524.

Freire, P. (1968). *Pedagogy of the oppressed.* New York: Continuum Press.

Freire, P., & Shor, I. (1987). *A pedagogy for liberation: Dialogues on transforming education.* South Hadley, MA: Bergin & Garvey.

Gilligan, C. (1982). *In a different voice: Psychological theory and women's development.* Cambridge, MA: Harvard University Press.

Ginott, H. G. (1965). *Between parent and child.* New York: Avon.

Golding, W. (1954). *Lord of the flies.* New York: Putnam.

Goodlad, J. I. (1984). *A place called school: Prospects for the future.* New York: McGraw-Hill.

Goodlad, J. I. (1990). Better teachers for our nation's schools. *Phi Delta Kappan, 72*(3), 184-194.

Gordon, T. (1974). *Teacher effectiveness training.* New York: P. H. Wyden.

Grant, C. A., & Zeichner, K. M. (1981). Inservice support for first year teachers: The state of the scene. *Journal of Research and Development in Education, 14*(2), 99-111.

Gray, W. A., & Gray, M. M. (Eds.). (1986). *Mentoring: A comprehensive annotated bibliography of important references.* Vancouver, BC: International Association for Mentoring.

Grumet, M. R. (1988). *Bitter milk: Women and teaching.* Amherst: University of Massachusetts Press.

Haberman, M. (1992). Should college youth be prepared for teaching? *Educational Forum, 57*(1), 30-36.

Hawthorne, N. (1981). *The scarlet letter.* New York: Bantam. (Original work published 1850)

Holt, J. (1967). *How children learn.* New York: Dell.

Jersild, A. T. (1955). *When teachers face themselves.* New York: Teachers College Press.

Johnson, D. W., & Johnson, R. T. (1975). *Learning together and alone.* Englewood Cliffs, NJ: Prentice Hall.

Joyce, B. R., & Showers, B. (1983). *Power in staff development through research on training.* Alexandria, VA: Association for Supervision and Curriculum Development.

Katz, L. G., Morpurgo, J., Asper, L., & Wolf, R. L. (1974). Advisory approach to inservice training. *Journal of Teacher Education, 25,* 154-159.

Keyes, K. (1982). *Hundredth monkey.* Coos Bay, OR: Love Line Books.

Kohlberg, L., & Mayer, R. (1972). Development as the aim of education. *Harvard Educational Review, 42*(4), 449-496.

Kram, K. E. (1985). *Mentoring at work: Developing relationships in organizational life.* Glenview, IL: ScottForesman.

Lee, H. (1960). *To kill a mockingbird.* Philadelphia: Lippincott.

Locke, L. F. (1984). Research on teaching teachers: Where are we now? *Journal of Teaching in Physical Education* (Monograph 2).

London, J. (1914). *Call of the wild.* Philadelphia: D. McKay.

Lortie, D. C. (1975). *Schoolteacher: A sociological study.* Chicago: University of Chicago Press.

Marlowe, C. (1962). *Doctor Faustus.* Cambridge, MA: Harvard University Press. (Original work published 1604)

McCullers, C. (1967). *The heart is a lonely hunter.* Boston: Houghton Mifflin.

Miller, A. (1953). *The crucible.* New York: Viking.

Munby, H. (1982). The place of teachers' beliefs in research on teacher thinking and decision making, and an alternative methodology. *Instructional Science, 11,* 201-225.

Nason, H. D. (1986). *Maintenance of change in teaching practices sub-sequent to staff development: Do follow-up activities make a differ-ence?* Unpublished doctoral dissertation, Vanderbilt Univer-sity, Nashville, TN.

Newman, C. R. (1980). *The advisor as teacher supporter.* Unpublished doctoral dissertation, University of Massachusetts School of Education at Amherst.

Orwell, G. (1945). *Animal farm.* Bergenfield, NJ: New American Library.

Portuges, C. (1985). The spectacle of gender: Cinema and psyche. In M. Culley & C. Portuges (Eds.), *Gendered subjects: The dynamics of feminist teaching* (pp. 183-194). Boston: Routledge Kegan Paul.

Raymond, J. C. (1985). Women's studies: A knowledge of one's own. In M. Culley & C. Portuges (Eds.), *Gendered subjects: The dynam-ics of feminist teaching* (pp. 49-63). Boston: Routledge Kegan Paul.

Rich, A. (1979). *On lies, secrets, and silence.* New York: Norton.

Rich, Y. (1990). Ideological impediments to instructional innovation: The case of cooperative learning. *Teaching and Teacher Education, 6*(1), 81-91.

Rifkin, J. (1985). Teaching mediation: A feminist perspective on the study of law. In M. Culley & C. Portuges (Eds.), *Gendered sub-jects: The dynamics of feminist teaching* (pp. 96-107). Boston: Routledge Kegan Paul.

Rogers, C. R. (1951). *Client-centered therapy: Its current practice, impli-cations, and theory.* Boston: Houghton Mifflin.

Rogers, C. R. (1973). The characteristics of a helping relationship. In D. L. Avila, A. W. Combs, & W. W. Purkey (Eds.), *The helping relationship sourcebook* (pp. 2-18). Boston: Allyn & Bacon.

Rogers, C. R. (1977). *Carl Rogers on personal power.* New York: Dela-corte.

Ross, E. W. (1986, November). *Becoming a social studies teacher: Teacher education and the development of preservice teacher perspectives.* Paper presented at the annual meeting of the National Council for the Social Studies, New York.

Rossman, G., Corbett, H. D., & Firestone, W. A. (1988). *Change and effectiveness in schools: A cultural perspective.* Albany: State Uni-versity of New York Press.

Ruddick, J. (1987). Partnership supervision as a basis for the pro-fessional development of new and experienced teachers. In

M. F. Wideen & I. Andrews (Eds.), *Staff development for school improvement: A focus on the teacher* (pp. 129-141). New York: Falmer.

Sarason, S. B. (1982). *The culture of the school and the problem of change.* Boston: Allyn & Bacon.

Schniedewind, N., & Davidson, E. (1987). *Cooperative learning, cooperative lives: A sourcebook of learning activities for building a peaceful world.* Dubuque, IA: William C. Brown.

Sennett, R., & Cobb, J. (1972). *The hidden injuries of class.* New York: Random House.

Sergiovanni, T. H., & Starratt, R. J. (1979). *Supervision: Human perspectives.* New York: McGraw-Hill.

Sharan, S. (1984). *Cooperative learning in the classroom: Research in desegregated schools.* Hillsdale, NJ: Lawrence Erlbaum.

Shelley, M. W. (1984). *Frankenstein.* Berkeley: University of California Press. (Original work published 1818)

Sizer, T. R. (1984). *Horace's compromise: The dilemma of the American high school.* Boston: Houghton Mifflin.

Snoek, D. (1985). A male feminist in a women's college classroom. In M. Culley & C. Portuges (Eds.), *Gendered subjects: The dynamics of feminist teaching* (pp. 136-143). Boston: Routledge Kegan Paul.

Sorcinelli, M. D. (1978). *The teaching consultation process: A study of personal and professional development in faculty.* Unpublished doctoral dissertation, University of Massachusetts at Amherst.

Stockton, F. (1893). The lady or the tiger. In *"The lady or the tiger" and other stories* (pp. 1-10). New York: Scribner.

Tabachnick, B. R., & Zeichner, K. M. (1984). The impact of the student teaching experience on the development of teacher perspectives. *Journal of Teacher Education, 35,* 28-36.

Tabachnick, B. R., & Zeichner, K. M. (1985). *The development of teacher perspectives: Final report.* Madison: Wisconsin Center for Education Research.

Twain, M. (1981). *The adventures of Huckleberry Finn.* New York: Bantam. (Original work published 1884)

Tyson, H. (1994). *Who will teach the children? Progress and resistance in teacher education.* San Francisco: Jossey-Bass.

Wells, K. (1984, February). *Teacher socialization in the educational organization: A review of the literature.* Paper presented at the annual meeting of the Western Speech Communication Association, Seattle, WA.

Welty, E. (1982). The worn path. In D. Hall (Ed.), *To read literature: Fiction, poetry, drama* (pp. 56-62). New York: Holt, Rinehart & Winston.

Wideen, M. F., & Andrews, I. (Eds.). (1987). *Staff development for school improvement: A focus on the teacher.* New York: Falmer.

Wigginton, E. (1985). *Sometimes a shining moment: The foxfire experience. Twenty years teaching in a high school classroom.* Garden City, NY: Anchor.

Williams, J. A., & Williamson, K. M. (1994, February). *A university model of support for novice teachers: Success, struggles, and limitations.* Paper presented at the annual meeting of the American Association of Colleges of Teacher Education, Chicago.

Zeichner, K. M. (1980, April). *Key processes in the socialization of student teachers: Limitations and consequences of oversocialized conceptions of teacher socialization.* Paper presented at the annual meeting of the American Educational Research Association, Boston.

Zeichner, K. M., & Liston, D. P. (1987). Teaching student teachers to reflect. *Harvard Educational Review, 57*(1), 23-48.

Index